I0412347

Retrocausality

Experiments and Theory

Antonella Vannini & Ulisse Di Corpo

www.sintropia.it

Copyright © 2011 Antonella Vannini & Ulisse Di Corpo

ISBN: 9781520275956

CONTENTS

INTRODUCTION

The notion of energy comes from the fact that physical systems possess a quantity that can be turned into a force.

This quantity can take the form of heat, mass, electromagnetism, potential, kinetic, nuclear and chemical energy.

Despite the fact that it is used and studied

"it is important to realize that in physics today we have no knowledge of what energy is."[1]

The energy-mass relation:

$$E = mc^2$$

that we all associate with Einstein, was first published by Oliver Heaviside in 1890[2], then by Henri Poincaré in 1900[3] and by Olinto De Pretto in 1904[4]. Olinto De Pretto presented it at the *Reale Istituto Veneto di Scienze* in an essay with a preface by the astronomer and senator Giovanni Schiaparelli.

---

[1] Feynman R (1965), *The Feynman Lectures on Physics*, California Institute of Technology, 1965, 3.

[2] Auffray J.P., *Dual origin of E=mc2*:http://arxiv.org/pdf/physics/0608289.pdf

[3] Poincaré H,. *Arch. néerland. sci.* 2, 5, 252-278 (1900).

[4] De Pretto O., *Lettere ed Arti*, LXIII, II, 439-500 (1904), Reale Istituto Veneto di Scienze.

It seems that this equation has come to Einstein through his father Hermann who was responsible for the lighting systems in Verona and who, as director of the *"Privilegiata Impresa Elettrica Einstein"*, had frequent contacts with the Fonderia De Pretto that produced the turbines for electricity.

However, the $E=mc^2$ does not take into account the momentum, which is also a form of energy and in 1905 Einstein added the momentum (p), thus obtaining the energy-momentum-mass equation:

$$E^2=m^2c^4+p^2c^2$$

Since energy is squared (E^2) and in the momentum (p) there is time a square root is used and there are two solutions: negative time energy and positive time energy.

E^{-t}, *negative time energy, manifests as converging energy*

E^{+t}, *positive time energy, manifests as diverging energy*

Positive time energy implies causality, whereas negative time energy implies _retrocausality_: the future that acts back into the past.

This was considered impossible and to solve this paradox Einstein removed the momentum, given the fact that it is practically equal to zero when compared to the speed of light (c). In this way, we return to the $E=mc^2$.

However, in 1924 the spin of the electron was discovered. The spin is an angular momentum, a rotation of the electron on itself at a speed close to that of light. Since this speed is very high, the momentum cannot be considered equal to zero and in quantum mechanics the energy-momentum-mass equation must be used with its uncomfortable dual solution.

The first equation that combined relativity and quantum mechanics was formulated in 1926 by Oskar Klein and Walter Gordon and has two time solutions: advanced and delayed waves. Advanced waves were rejected, since they imply retrocausality which was considered impossible.

The second equation, formulated in 1928 by Paul Dirac, also has two time solutions: electrons and neg-electrons (now called positron). The existence of positrons was proved in 1932 by Carl Andersen.

Shortly after Wolfgang Pauli and Carl Gustav Jung formulated the theory of synchronicities. Starting from the dual time solution they came to the conclusion that reality is supercausal, with causes acting from the past and synchronicities acting from the future.

In 1933 Heisenberg, who had a strong charismatic personality and a leading position in the institutions and academia, declared the backward in time solution impossible. From that moment, anyone who ventures into the study of the backward in time solution is discredited, loses the academic position, the ability to publish and to talk at conferences.

However, in the laboratories of physics it seems impossible to test retrocausality, since:

1. according to Wheeler's and Feynman's electrodynamics, all the time-symmetric models lead to predictions identical with those of conventional electrodynamics. For this reason it is impossible to distinguish between time-symmetric results and conventional results.[5]

2. In his transactional interpretations of quantum mechanics, John Cramer states that *"Nature, in a very subtle way, may be engaging in backward in time handshaking. But the use of this mechanism is not available to experimental investigators even at the microscopic level. The completed transaction erases all advanced effects, so that no advanced wave signaling is possible. The future can affect the past only very indirectly, by offering possibilities for transactions."*[6]

Luigi Fantappiè studied pure mathematics at the Normale di Pisa, the most exclusive Italian University, where he had been classmate of Enrico Fermi. He was well known and appreciated among physicists to the point that in 1951 Oppenheimer invited him to become a member of the

[5] Wheeler J.A. and Feynman R.P. (1949), *Classical Electrodynamics in Terms of Direct Interparticle Action*, Reviews of Modern Physics 21 (3): 425–433.
[6] Cramer J.G. (1986),The *Transactional Interpretation of Quantum Mechanics*, Reviews of Modern Physics, Vol. 58: 647-688.

exclusive Institute for Advanced Study in Princeton and work directly with Einstein.

As a mathematician Fantappiè could not accept that Heisenberg had rejected half of the solutions of the fundamental equations and in 1941, while listing the properties of the forward and backward in time energy, Fantappiè discovered that the forward in time energy is governed by the law of *entropy*, whereas the backward in time energy is governed by a complementary law that he named *syntropy*, combining the Greek words *syn* which means converging and *tropos* which means tendency.

Entropy is the tendency towards energy dissipation, the famous second law of thermodynamics, also known as the law of heat death. On the contrary, syntropy is the tendency towards energy concentration, increase in differentiation, complexity and structures. These are the mysterious properties of life!

In 1944 Fantappiè published the book *"Principi di una Teoria Unitaria del Mondo Fisico e Biologico"* (Unitary Theory of the Physical and Biological World) in which he suggested that the physical-material world is governed by entropy and causality, while the biological world is governed by syntropy and retrocausality.[7]

We cannot see the future and therefore retrocausality is invisible! The dual energy solution suggests the presence of a visible reality (causal and entropic) and an invisible one (retrocausal and syntropic).

---

[7] Fantappiè L., *Principi di una teoria unitaria del mondo fisico e biologico.* Humanitas Nova, Roma 1944.

The first law of thermodynamics states that energy is a unity that cannot be created or destroyed, but only transformed, and the energy-momentum-mass equation shows that this unity has two components: entropy and syntropy. We can therefore write:

$$1 = Entropy + Syntropy \qquad Syntropy = 1 - Entropy$$

where syntropy is the complement of entropy! Life lies between these two components: one visible and the other invisible, one entropic and the other syntropic, and this can be portrayed using a seesaw.

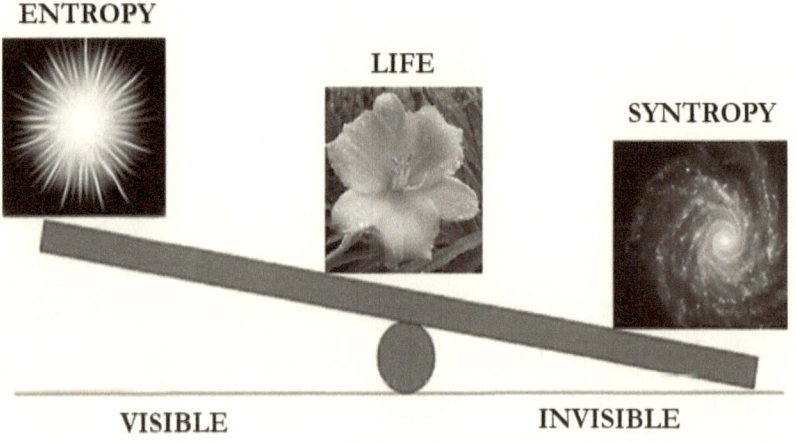

We cannot see the future and therefore syntropy is invisible!

An example is provided by gravity. We continually experience gravity, but we cannot see it. According to the dual time energy solution gravity is a force that diverges backwards in time and, for us moving forward in time, is a converging force. The fact that gravity is invisible is known to all, but that it diverges from the future is known to few.

Can we prove it?

Yes, and it's quite simple. If gravity propagates from the future its speed must exceed that of light. Tom van Flandern, an American astronomer specialized in celestial mechanics, developed a series of procedures to measure the speed of gravity propagation[8,9,10].

In the case of light, which has a constant speed of about 300,000 kilometers per second, we observe the phenomenon of aberration. Sunlight takes about 500 seconds to reach the Earth. So when it arrives, we see the Sun in the sky position it occupied 500 seconds before. This difference is equivalent to about 20 seconds of arc, a large amount for astronomers. Sunlight strikes the Earth from a slightly shifted angle and this shift is called aberration.

If the speed of gravity propagation were limited, one would expect to observe aberration in gravity measurements. Gravity should be maximum in the position occupied by the Sun when gravity left the Sun. Instead, observations indicate

[8] Van Flander T. (1996), *Possible New Properties of Gravity*, Astrophysics and Space Science 244:249-261.
[9] Van Flander T. (1998), *The Speed of Gravity What the Experiments Say*, Physics Letters A 250:1-11.
[10] Van Flandern T. and Vigier J.P. (1999), *The Speed of Gravity – Repeal of the Speed Limit*, Foundations of Physics 32:1031-1068.

that there is no detectable delay in the propagation of gravity from the Sun to the Earth. The direction of the gravitational attraction of the Sun is exactly towards the position in which the Sun is, not towards a previous position, and this shows that the speed of propagation of gravity is infinite.

Instant propagation of gravity can only be explained if we accept that gravity is a force that diverges backwards in time, a physical manifestations of syntropy.

Fantappiè failed to prove his theory, since the experimental method requires the manipulation of causes before observing their effects.

Recently, random event generators (REG) have become available. These systems allow to perform experiments in which causes are manipulated after their effects: in the future.

The first experimental study on retrocausality, by Dean Radin of the ION (Institute of Noetic Sciences)[11], measured heart rate, skin conductance and blood pressure in subjects who were presented with blank images for 5 seconds followed by images that, based on a random event generator, could be neutral or emotional. The results showed a significant activation of the parameters of the autonomic nervous system, before the presentation of emotional images.

In 2003, Spottiswoode and May, of the Cognitive Science Laboratory, replicated this experiment by performing a

---

[11] Radin D.I. (1997), *Unconscious perception of future emotions: An experiment in presentiment*, Journal of Scientific Exploration, 11(2): 163-180.

series of controls to study possible artifacts and alternative explanations. The results confirmed those already obtained by Radin[12]. Similar results were found by other authors, such as McCraty, Atkinson and Bradley[13], Radin and Schlitz[14] and May, Paulinyi and Vassy[15], always using the parameters of the autonomic nervous system.

Daryl Bem, psychologist and professor at the Cornell University, describes nine classic experiments conducted in the retrocausal mode in order to get the effects first rather than after the stimulus. For example, in a priming experiment, the subject is asked to judge whether the image is positive (pleasant) or negative (unpleasant) by pressing a button as quickly as possible. The reaction time is recorded.[16]

Just before the positive or negative image, a word is presented briefly, below the threshold so that it is not perceptible at a conscious level. This word is called *"prime"* and it has been observed that subjects tend to respond more quickly when the prime is congruent with the following

[12] Spottiswoode P (2003) e May E, *Skin Conductance Prestimulus Response: Analyses, Artifacts and a Pilot Study*, Journal of Scientific Exploration, 2003, 17(4): 617-641.
[13] McCratly R (2004), Atkinson M e Bradely RT, *Electrophysiological Evidence of Intuition: Part 1*, Journal of Alternative and Complementary Medicine; 2004, 10(1): 133-143.
[14] Radin DI (2005) e Schlitz MJ, *Gut feelings, intuition, and emotions: An exploratory study*, Journal of Alternative and Complementary Medicine, 2005, 11(4): 85-91.
[15] May EC (2005), Paulinyi T e Vassy Z, *Anomalous Anticipatory Skin Conductance Response to Acoustic Stimuli: Experimental Results and Speculation about a Mechanism*, The Journal of Alternative and Complementary Medicine. August 2005, 11(4): 695-702.
[16] Bem D (2011), *Feeling the future: Experimental evidence for anomalous retroactive influences on cognition and affect*, Journal of Personality and Social Psychology, Jan 31, 2011.

image, whether it is a positive or negative image, while the reactions become slower when they are not congruent, for example when the word is positive while the image is negative.

In retro-priming experiments, the usual stimulus procedure takes place later, rather than before the subject responds, based on the hypothesis that this "inverse" procedure can retrocausally influence the answers. The experiments were conducted on more than a thousand subjects and showed retrocausal effects with statistical significance of a possibility on 134,000,000,000 of being mistaken when affirming the existence of the retrocausal effect.

Syntropy explains these results in the following way:

"Since life feeds on syntropy, and syntropy flows backward in time, the parameters of the autonomic nervous system that support vital functions must react in advance to future stimuli."

As part of her doctoral thesis in cognitive psychology, Antonella Vannini conducted four experiments using heart rate (HR) measurements to study the retrocausal effect.

Each experimental trial was divided into 3 phases:

Phase 1				Phase 2	Phase 3
Presentation of stimuli and measurement of heart rate				Choice	Random selection
Blue	Green	Red	Yellow	Blue/Green/Red/Yellow	Red
					Target
4 seconds	4 seconds	4 seconds	4 seconds		Feedback

1. *Phase 1,* in which 4 colors were displayed one after the other on the computer screen. The subject had to look at these colors and during their presentation the heart rate was measured.
2. *Phase 2,* in which an image with 4 colored bars was displayed and the subject had to try to guess the color that the computer would have selected.
3. *Phase 3,* in which the computer randomly selected the color and showed it full screen.

The hypothesis was that in the case of a retrocausal effect differences should be observed among the heart rates measured in phase 1 in correlation with the target color selected in phase 3 from the computer.

In the absence of the retrocausal effect, the heart rates differences associated with each color of the target stimulus should have varied around the zero value (0).

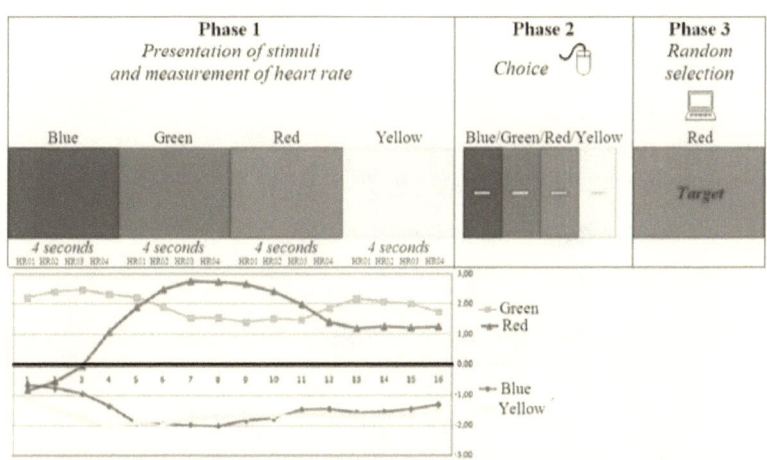

Retrocausal effect observed on a subject

15

Instead, a marked difference was observed!

In some subjects the heart rate increased when the target color was blue and decreased when the target was green. In others exactly the opposite was observed.

Performing data analysis within each subject, the retrocausal effect was clear. But, when the analysis was conducted in a classical way, adding the effects observed among several subjects, opposite effects canceled.

This suggested that when studying retrocausal effects parametric statistical techniques such as analysis of variance (ANOVA) or Student's t are not suitable, while nonparametric techniques such as Chi Square and Fisher's exact test are appropriate.

This is consistent with the division made by Stuart Mill in the methodology of differences and methodology of concomitant variations.[17]

Mill showed that causality can be studied using:

1. The methodology of differences: *"If an element of difference is introduced in two initially similar groups, the differences that are observed can only be attributed to this single element that was introduced."*
2. The methodology of concomitant variations: *"When two phenomena vary concomitantly, one may be the cause of the other or both are united by the same cause."*

---

[17] Stuart Mill, *A System of Logic*, 1843.

The study of syntropic phenomena requires the use of the methodology of concomitant variations[18] where the information is translated into dichotomous variables (yes/no). This allows to analyze together quantitative and qualitative, objective and subjective information and to manage an unlimited number of variables simultaneously.

---

[18] See: www.amazon.com/dp/1520326637 and
www.sintropia.it/sintropia.ds.zip

EXPERIMENTAL DESIGN

In order to test retrocausal effects it is necessary to use Random Event Generators.

In a random sequence each term is totally independent from the previous and following terms, no rule links different parts of the sequence. This condition is known as unpredictability of random sequences and it is referred to as "lack of memory": the process of random selection does not recall any information about the values which were selected previously and cannot be used for the prediction of the values which will be selected in the future.

Random sequences imply:

1. *Unpredictability.* The knowledge of any portion of the random sequence does not provide useful information in order to predict the outcome of any other element of the sequence. In other words, the knowledge of the first k values does not provide any element in order to predict the value k+1: this property is called unpredictability.
2. *Equiprobability.* A sequence is random if in each position each value has the same probability to be selected. In the case of a dice, each side has the same probability to be selected. Similarly, equal probability is expected when using a coin: during each tossing heads and tails have the same probability to show. Equiprobability implies

independent sequences as it requires that the outcome of each selection is independent from any previous selection.

3. *Irregularity*. Unpredictability requires random sequences to be irregular and not repetitive.

4. *Absence of order*. In random sequences no type of structure or order can be detected.

The basic difference between causal and random can be traced back to the fact that causal events can be predicted, whereas random events cannot be predicted. A random sequence can be defined as a sequence that no cognitive process will ever be able to predict.

- Pseudorandom and random

Computer languages usually use the word random to identify the instruction which starts the algorithm for the random selection of numbers. In the experiments described in this book the Delphi-Pascal programming language was used. Delphi-Pascal has a predefined random sequence of 2^{32} numbers which can be assessed through a pointer which can be defined by the user or by the value of the built-in clock. Delphi-Pascal uses the following instructions:

1. *Randomize* reads the value of the built-in clock and uses this value as the pointer to the predefined random sequence;

2. *Random* reads the value of the predefined sequence using the pointer selected by the randomize instruction.

The user can also define a personalized pointer. This option is generally used to encrypt information. Using the same pointer the random sequence will always be the same.

Random sequences produced by computers are named pseudorandom since loops require always the same processing time and the new random value will therefore be determined by the previous one.

The problem with random sequences generated by computers arises when the randomize procedure is recalled in a loop since random numbers will be determined by the first value which was selected: the first value determines the second value, and so on, and the condition of independency between different terms is lost.

Usually the fact that computers produce pseudorandom sequences is considered insignificant. However, in experiments which want to test retrocausality, and which are based on the assumption of unpredictability, a pseudo-random sequence would inevitably be an artifact.

Luckily the solution is relatively simple. The problem arises from the fact that the period of the loops is always the same. In order to overcome this problem, obtaining in this way pure random sequences, it is necessary to use loops which are based on unpredictable periods of time. This condition can be easily met when an external, unpredictable factor, is inserted in the loop and modifies its execution time.

In the experiments described in this book subjects were

asked to try to guess the color that the computer will select, pressing a button: the reaction time of the subject is unpredictable. In this way, the unpredictable reaction time of the subject, makes loops time become unpredictable, and the value read from the built-in clock of the computer becomes independent from the other values, the independence is restored and the sequence becomes totally unpredictable: perfectly random.

- Choice of the heart rate frequency device

Before starting the experiments (late 2007), an assessment of heart rate and skin conductance measuring devices was carried out. With most devices it was difficult to associate the measurements with the exact time, since:

1. they used a different clock from the one used by the computer;
2. data did not consider the time required to produce the measurements;
3. built-in software did not satisfy the synchronization requirements;
4. proprietary software did not allow to access directly the device.

In order to try to overcome these difficulties a laboratory in North Italy provided some devices, but still it was impossible to establish a satisfactory synchronization between the measuring devices and the stimuli which were presented on the PC monitor.

In December 2007 the assessment was extended to devices used in the field of sports training. Most devices showed the following limits:

1. Heart rate measurements are stored in a wrist watch, using a different clock from the one used to conduct the experiment.
2. The information is stored without any compensation for the delay due to the measurement.
3. Some devices showed errors in the measurement.

After a long evaluation, the "home training" device produced by SUUNTO (www.suunto.com), was chosen. This system includes a thorax belt for measuring heart rate parameters, and a USB interface (PC-POD) which receives measurements by radio, using digital coded signals (which eliminate any possibility of interference) directly on the PC on which the experiment was carried out and using in this way the same clock of the PC.

The SUUNTO heart monitor device saves the heart frequency information every second, together with time information (year, month, day, hour, minute and second) provided by the PC clock. The measurement is relative to the average value during the second and it is saved compensating the delay due to the time necessary to perform the measurement and to process the information. The heart rate data time, saved in the file, is therefore synchronized with the data saved by the software which governed the execution of the experiment.

The heart rate information was saved as an integer number, without any decimal values. The technical support unit of SUUNTO was contacted in Helsinki and gave full cooperation sending all the necessary documentation, software and .ddl libraries. SUUNTO underlined that synchronization and precision of measurements are diverging parameters. A precise synchronization diminishes the precision of the measurement. An integer value of the heart rate, provided every second, can be considered an excellent measurement.

The SUUNTO "home training" device was developed in order to monitor sports training activities and can be used in the most extreme conditions, for example underwater. It does not require the use of gel in order to receive the heart signal and its use is extremely simple. It does not require the presence of an assistant in the same room in which the experiment is carried out. The only limit was observed in cold weathers when the skin gets dry and this limited the possibility to measure the heart rate parameter.

- Performance of the SUUNTO heart rate device

Before starting the experiments the synchronization of the SUUNTO heart rate device with the built in clock of the PC was assessed. The heart rate information is shown in "real time" on the PC monitor and it is also saved in a file.

1. In *real time* on the PC monitor it was observed that: when the signal is deactivated (moving the thorax belt away from the chest of the subject) the data flow stops after 5 seconds; when the signal is reactivated (moving the thorax belt back on the chest of the subject) the data flow reappears after 2 seconds.

2. In the data saved in the *file* it was observed that: when the signal is deactivated (moving the thorax belt away from the chest of the subject) the last measurement is kept for 3 seconds; when the signal is reactivated (moving the thorax belt back on the chest of the subject) the measurement reappears immediately.

In other words, the delay in the measurements shown in "real time" on the PC monitor is approximately of 2 seconds, whereas in the data file the delay was corrected and the measurements were associated to the exact time.

In the data file the measurement of the heart rate is associated with the time of the clock of the computer (year, month, day, hour, minute and second). A control carried out during the statistical analyses showed that the measurements are relative to the second shown by the clock, therefore a measurement associated with 14.13'.25" has been calculated starting at 14.13'.25".000 and ending at 14.13'.25".999.

- Stimuli

Several experimental designs were tested and a design divided in 3 phases was chosen:

1. In the *presentation phase*: 4 stimuli were shown individually on the PC monitor and the heart rate was measured.
2. In the *choice phase*: stimuli were shown together on the PC monitor and the subject tried to guess which one the computer will select.
3. In the *random selection phase* the computer selects one of the 4 stimuli (target stimulus), using a random procedure, and showed it on the PC monitor, full screen.

The hypothesis is that in the event of retrocausality heart rate measurements in phase 1 (the presentation phase) should be significantly different among target images (those which will be selected randomly by the computer in phase 3).

The first experiments used stimuli made of black bars placed horizontally, vertically and diagonally on a white background. Data analyses did not show any significant difference among heart rates measured in phase 1.

The hypothesis was therefore analyzed in more depth and it was found that the "syntropy theory" posits that retrocausality is mediated by emotions/feelings and, therefore, in order to assess differences in heart rates measured in phase 1 stimuli in phase 3 should arise feelings. Following this indication it was decided to use 4 elementary colors: blue, green, red and yellow. Using colors a strong difference in heart frequencies in phase 1 was observed in concomitance to the target shown in phase 3.

In the first experiments in phase 1, stimuli were presented for 4 seconds each and heart rate was measured each second.

Phase 1				Phase 2	Phase 3
Presentation of stimuli and measurement of heart rate				Choice	Random selection
Blue	Green	Red	Yellow	Blue/Green/Red/Yellow	Red
					Target
4 seconds	4 seconds	4 seconds	4 seconds		Feedback
HR01 HR02 HR03 HR04	HR01 HR02 HR03 HR04	HR01 HR02 HR03 HR04	HR01 HR02 HR03 HR04		

During the experiment two software were active:

1. The SUUNTO Training Monitor 2.2.0 software which coupled each heart rate measurement with the date and second of the clock of the computer. Data was stored in a file in a directory created by the SUUNTO software.

2. A software developed using Delphi Pascal which was used for the presentation of stimuli. Stimuli were presented exactly at the turn of the second, with the precision of milliseconds, obtaining in this way the highest synchronization between the data stored by the SUUNTO software and stimuli presented by the computer. This last program saved data about the presentation in phase 1, the choice and reaction time of

the subject in phase 2, and the random selection of the computer in phase 3, in a different directory from the one used by the SUUNTO program. Each event was associated with the exact moment (year, month, day, hour, minute, second and millisecond).

At the end of the experiment the two files were merged (using the time information) obtaining in this way the file which was then used for the data analyses.

- Additive effects and statistical analyses

Analysis of variance (ANOVA) is usually required by scientific journals. ANOVA divides the observed variance in treatment variability (between groups) and error variability (within groups). The ratio of the treatment variability and the error variability produces a value, F, of which the statistical distribution is known and from which the value of the statistical significance of the effect is obtained. Requirements of ANOVA are:

1. *Homoscedasticity*. The variance of groups should be the same. The greater variability of one group results in a false statistical significances.
2. *Additive effects*. When effects are not additive the error variability tends to be greater and statistical significances are lost.

FIRST THREE EXPERIMENTS

The experimental trial is divided into 3 phases: in the presentation phase stimuli are shown individually on the PC monitor and heart rate is measured; in the choice phase stimuli are shown together on the PC monitor and the subject tries to guess which one will be selected by the computer; in the random selection phase the computer selects one of the 4 stimuli, using a random procedure, and shows it on the PC full screen (target stimulus).

The hypothesis of the experiment is that in the event of retrocausality, heart rates (HR) measured in phase 1 (the presentation phase) should be significantly different according to the target color selected and shown by the computer in phase 3.

Experimental conditions were gradually changed in order to understand the characteristics of the effect.

1. The first experiment used in phase 1 the sequence: blue, green, red and yellow. The sample was of 24 subjects. Results showed strong effects associated to the blue and green targets.
2. The second experiment was devised in order to answer the following questions: The retrocausal effect is observed only on blue and green targets? The retrocausal effect is observed only when using colors? The retrocausal effect is observed only when the computer shows the target? In this experiment the effect was

observed also associated to red and yellow targets and when numbers were used instead of colors. The effect disappeared when targets were not shown.

3. A third experiment was performed in which the target presentation was removed randomly. When the target was shown strong differences were observed associated to target colors in phase 1, whereas when the target was not shown these differences disappeared. This control eliminates the possibility of a forward-in-time effect.

- Data analysis

In the first experiment, stimuli were shown in phase 1 for 4 seconds each. Heart rate data was associated to each second and data analysis showed:

1. Strong statistically significant effects on all the colors, when the analyses were conducted within each subject.
2. Effects remained significant only on some colors when the analysis was carried out on the totality of the subjects.

The fact that the effect showed only on some colors was initially attributed to specific characteristics of these colors, but it was then understood that effects vanished when the analysis was carried out globally as a consequence of the fact that the effect can have different directions and they cannot be summed. Each subject presented a characteristic pattern in the heart rate frequency. For example, some subjects showed an increase in the heart rate frequency in phase 1 when the target color in phase 3 was blue, and a decrease in the heart rate frequency when the target was green. Other subjects showed a pattern which was exactly the opposite. When the analysis was carried out adding the effects among all the subjects, opposite effects cancelled and no effect was detectable.

In the second experiment controls were made modifying the sequence of presentation of colors and it was discovered that the effect appeared on all the colors.

In the third experiment statistical analysis used also the Chi Square index. It was discovered that the effect could be observed on all the colors.

It was understood that the absence of the effect, randomly on some colors, was the consequence of the requirement of ANOVA and of Student's. When the effect is not directional, ANOVA and Student's t cannot be used since adding the effects results in a null effect.

Nonparametric statistics, operates on frequencies and each value has the same weight. Outliers (out of scale values) do not lead to false statistical results, and opposite effects do not cancel each other.

The fourth experiment used only nonparametric statistics and results were strong and robust (repeatable).

Often in the field of psychology and neurosciences effects are non-directional and the use of ANOVA is therefore misleading.

But, historical reasons seems to have made ANOVA a must:

1. ANOVA is easy to calculate, even without a computer. Before the advent of computers ANOVA was therefore the only option.
2. Experimental research in psychology is focused on animal experimentation. In this field it is possible to use ANOVA correctly because it is easy to have homogeneous samples and effects are usually directional and can be added.

- Experiment n. 1

Each trial of the experiment was divided in 3 phases.

1. *Presentation phase*: 4 colors were shown for 4 seconds each. The first one was blue, the second one green, the third red and the fourth yellow. The subject was asked to look at the colors. For each color 4 measurements of the heart rate were saved: one each second. The presentation of the color was synchronized with the heart rate measurement. When necessary the synchronization was re-established showing a white image before the presentation of the first color in phase 1. The SUUNTO heart frequency device did not require any type of supervision. Subjects were alone while

conducting the experiment.

2. *Choice phase*: at the end of the presentation phase an image with 4 color bars was shown (blue, green, red and yellow) and the subject was asked to guess the target color that the computer would have selected in phase 3, by choosing the color bar using the mouse.

3. *Random selection of the target*: as soon as the subject chose the color bar the computer randomly selected the target color and showed it full-screen on the computer.

The experiment consisted of 20 trials and required approximately 7 minutes. Each subject was asked to repeat the experiment 3 times.

Hypothesis: *retrocausality should cause heart rate differences in phase 1 in association to target colors, which are selected by the computer in phase 3.*

Sample: the experiment was conducted on a sample of 24 subjects, with ages ranging from 15 to 75 years, 14 females and 10 males. Each subject performed the experiment 3 times, for a total time of slightly more than 20 minutes. Heart rate frequencies were measured 960 times for each subject, producing a sample which allowed to calculate statistical significance values also within each subject.

Data analysis. In this experiment data analysis was limited to heart rate frequencies measured in phase 1 in concomitance to the target color selected by the computer in phase 3. No differences were observed considering all the four colors together. An average value of the heart rate frequency of 80.94 when the color was targets and 80.97 when it was non-targets were obtained. When the analysis was conducted considering only one color at a time, strong differences were observed for the blue color (81.99 HR when target and 79.84 HR when non-target) and the green color (79.60 and 81.45). These differences correspond to a Student's t value of 10.74 for the blue color, and 8.81 for the green color. A Student's t value of 3.291 is statistically significant with p<0.001 (meaning that there is less than 1 probability in 1,000 to be wrong when stating that the difference is not a consequence of chance). A Student's t of 8.81 tells that the probability of being wrong is practically nil; it is therefore possible to state, with almost absolute certainty, that there is a relation between heart rate difference measured in phase 1 and the target color selected in phase 3 by the computer.

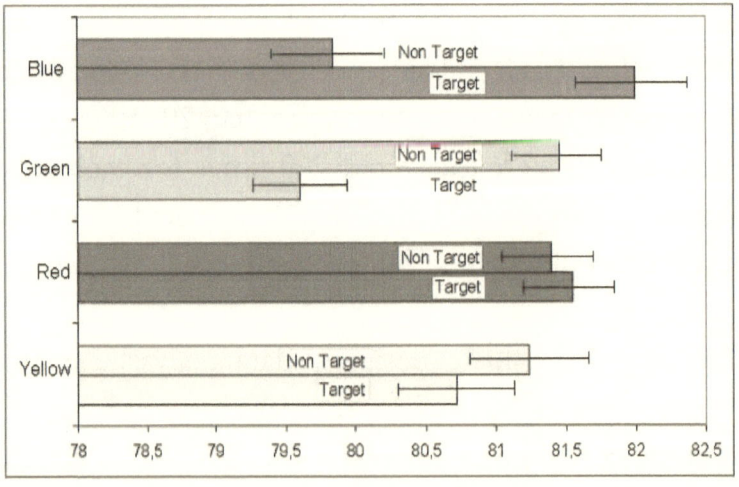

Although strong anticipatory heart rate reactions were observed, only a modest ability of guessing the target correctly was noticed. As a whole, 26.8% of the total guesses were correct, which is just slightly more than what it was expected by chance (25%). The rational conscious mind seems to access the anticipatory information of the heart only in a very limited way.

While most subjects showed a tendency towards higher heart rate frequencies when blue was target and lower heart rate frequencies when green was target, two subjects showed strong results in the opposite directions. Using Student's t and ANOVA when effects show in different directions they cancel each other, leading to a null effect. For colors red and yellow difference were observed in each subject, but these differences when added among subject resulted in a null effect.

Artifacts are systematic errors which lead to observe effects which do not exist. Sometimes artifacts are used intentionally by the experimenter in order to obtain the desired results; other times they consist in simple errors which produce accidental effects.

For example:

1. Errors linked to the experimental design are often caused by intervening variables which have not been

controlled. For instance, if in the experimental group the treatment is a substance, a drug in the form of a pill, while the control group does not receive any substance (no placebo pill), at the end of the experiment it will be impossible to say if the observed effect was caused by the substance in the pill or by the placebo effect of the pill.

2. Errors can be caused by non-homogeneous groups. Experiments are usually based on the comparison of groups, for example those who have received a drug and those who have received a placebo. The attribution to groups is randomized in order to distribute equally all the intervening variables of the population. However, in order to obtain homogeneous groups, randomization requires samples with a high number of subjects. Experiments are often conducted on small size samples, and intervening variables such as instruction, income, health, are not equally distributed among groups and this can cause differences among groups which are erroneously attributed to the "experimental treatment".

3. Errors linked with the measuring device happen when measurements are performed in systematically different ways among groups. When this happens differences observed can be the consequence of the different way used to perform measurements. In this case a systematic error of measuring is the cause of the effect.

4. Errors linked to statistical data analysis. Parametrical statistical analyses can be affected by extreme values. Sometimes the differences observed can be the

consequence of just one extreme value; furthermore, data might not comply with the requirements of the technique: this happens frequently with techniques which require the Gaussian distribution of data and results which can be added.

5. Errors can be linked to intentional manipulation of data by the experimenter in order to obtain the desired results.

In this first experiment the control of artifacts was the following:

1. Experimental design. The experiment is designed in such a way that the only element which differs is the color selected by the computer in phase 3: target or non-target. No other variables exist which might be associated to the target or non-target condition of the stimulus.

2. Sampling. Usually samples are divided in experimental and control group. In this experiment the distinction is between target and non-target stimuli and it is made within the same sample. Consequently this experimental design does not require randomization of subjects, since the two samples are identical. Measurements cannot be affected by sample differences.

3. Systematic measurement errors. The measurement of heart rate frequencies is performed in the same identical way for targets and non-target. Consequently no systematic error of measurement can be associated to

targets and non-targets.

4. Statistical analysis of data. Statistical analysis is always a very tricky field which hides problems of which the researcher might not be aware. In the last experiment statistical data analyses are performed using non parametric techniques, because it has become clear that the requirements of parametric statistical techniques cannot be met. Statistical artifacts are quite frequent when using parametric techniques, since they can lead to errors caused by extreme values and non-directional effects.

5. Intentional manipulation of data and results by the experimenter. Often, in order to participate to a conference, experimenters manipulate data sets and results. The doubt of data manipulation remains until results are not replicated by other researchers. Experiments described in this work are easy to replicate and other researchers have already replicated the results using various experimental designs.

The SUUNTO heart rate monitor has a range which goes from 30 heart rate beats per minute to 230 heart rate beats per minute, with a measuring error of ±0.5.

Errors distribute randomly around the mean values and this is known as the law of the sampling distribution of means: *"the mean of the means of samples, coincides with the mean of the population from which the samples were taken."*

While the single measurement of the heart rate has an error of ±0.5 beats per minute, when mean values are used this error decreases, since opposite measurements errors, when added, result in a null error, eliminating the distortion due to measuring errors.

The number of measurements performed in this study allows to consider significant mean values up to the fourth decimal digit. Generally speaking, the problem of the measuring device is taken into account when no statistical differences are observed and the problem could be related to the measurement device. In this study strong and statistically significant effects were observed and these results were replicated each time.

- Experiment n. 2

The second experiment was devised to answer the following questions:

1. Is the retrocausal effect limited to the blue and green targets?
2. Is the retrocausal effect limited to colors?
3. Is the retrocausal effect seen only when the computer shows the target in phase 3?

To answer these questions the experiment was organized in 5 different trials:

1. in 3 trials the sequence of the colors was varied in order to answer question n. 1;

2. in one trial instead of colors numbers were used, in order to answer question n. 2;
3. in one trial the target color was selected by the computer, but it was not shown, in order to answer question n. 3.

The effect was assessed in the form of differences between heart rates measured in phase 1.

The following hypothesis were formulated.

1. The retrocausal effect is expected in all the trials in which the target is shown. The presentation of the target is considered to be the cause of the heart rate differences.
2. The retrocausal effect is expected on all the colors. The hypothesis is that the retrocausal effect is mediated by feelings and it is believed that all colors, and also stimuli different from colors, such as numbers, can arouse feelings.

The experiment was divided in 5 trials, each one with a different sequence of colors and stimuli:

In the first trial, in phase 1 the sequence is blue, green, red and yellow and each color is shown for four seconds; in phase 2 these four colors come together and when the subject guesses, pressing on one of the colors, the computer selects the target color and shows it full screen (phase 3). A button then indicates the percentage of correct guesses; when pressed the next trial starts.

Trial n. 2 and n. 3 are similar to trial n. 1. The sequence of the colors is in trial 2 yellow, red, green and blue, and in trial 3 red, yellow, blue and green. In trial n. 4 the target color is selected by the computer but not shown, whereas in trial n. 5 numbers (1, 2, 3 and 4) are used instead of colors.

This sequence of 5 trials was repeated for 20 times, reaching a total of 100 trials for each subject, for a total length of the experiment of slightly more than 45 minutes. Heart rate was measured throughout all the experiment every second.

The sample was of 23 subjects, 14 females and 9 males, ranging from 16 to 61 years of age. For each color in phase 1 only one measurement of the heart rate was used in the statistical data analysis. The number of heart rate measurements is therefore 400 (for each subject) x 23 (subjects) = 9,200 (Total). The effect was studied using the Student's t test. In this experiment strong differences were observed, with Student's t values greater than 6.

Results show the effect for all the colors and not only for blue and green; the effect appears also when numbers, are used, but when the target is not shown the effect disappears.

Student's t test values are 5% statistically meaningful with values exceeding 1.96 and 1% with values exceeding 2.57.

When the target is not shown no statistically meaningful results were observed and this supports the fact that seeing the target is the cause of the retrocausal effect.

	Trial with colours			
	1	2	3	4
Blue	-	4.746	-3.455	-
Green	-	-	2.839	-
Red	-6.649	-	-	-
Yellow	5.623	-3.894	-	-

Student's t meaningful values

The fifth trial shows a strong effect (Student's t -5.7) only for the target number n. 4.

- Experiment n. 3

In the second experiment a grey screen instead of the target was shown in trial n. 4. This regularity could constitute an artifact. A third experiment was performed in which the grey screen was shown randomly. Results indicate that when the color target is shown strong differences are observed, whereas when the grey color is shown instead of the target color selected by the computer, these differences disappear. This control rules out the possibility that the effect can depend on forward-in-time causality.

Trials differ from the previous experiment in two ways:

1. the computer selects randomly if the target color will be shown or not;
2. the presentation time of colors in phase 1 was reduced from 4 seconds to 2 seconds each. This condition allowed to reduce the length of the experiment.

The experiment was intended to:

1. Verify again the retrocausal effect in phase 1.
2. Verify if the effect in phase 1 persists when the target is not shown. More precisely when the computer selects the target color (phase 3), but instead of showing it shows a grey screen.

The hypothesis is that when the target is not shown the retrocausal effect should disappear.

The experiment consisted of 100 trials per subject, of which slightly less than 1 out of 5 were without target. The sample consisted of 8 subjects. Trials without target were chosen randomly by the computer. On a total of 800 trials 151 were without target presentation. A total of 3,200 heart rate measurements (8 subjects x 100 trials x 4 stimuli) were used in the data analysis, 604 were without target and 2,596 with target. Even though the presentation time was reduced from 4 to 2 seconds the effect was strong for the blue and the yellow target colors. The effect was totally absent when the computer did not show the target color.

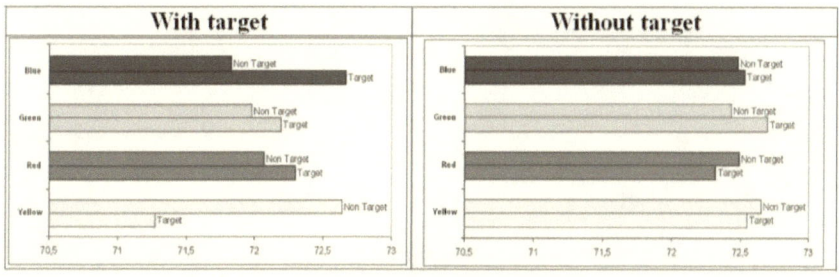

Average heart rate values

As in the previous experiments, a slight tendency towards guessing correctly was noticed (26% compared to 25%). This increase is not statistically significant, but it is interesting to note that in the first 50 trials 25.08% guesses were correct, whereas in the last 50 trials this percentage increased to 26.95%. This might suggest that people can be trained to use feelings with retrocausal information.

ROLE OF FEELINGS

Antonio Damasio[19] and Antoine Bechara[20] suggest a dual system of information processing, on which decision making would be based:

1. a *conscious* system, which uses reasoning in order to formulate decisions;
2. an *unconscious* system, which uses a different neurophysiological network in which Somatic Markers, which can be measured through skin conductance and heart rate frequencies, seem to play a key role.

This dual system recalls the syntropy hypothesis of a dual flow of information:

1. *cognitive*, which follow the classical flow of information, from the past to the future, based on the use of memory, learning and experience;
2. *feelings*, based on the perception of the future.

Studying neurological patients affected by decision making deficits, Damasio suggested the somatic markers (SM) hypothesis according to which feelings are part of the

---

[19] Damasio AR (1994), *Descarte's Error. Emotion, Reason, and the Human Brain*, Putnam Publishing, 1994.
[20] Bechara A (1997), Damasio H, Tranel D and Damasio AR (1997) *Deciding Advantageously before Knowing the Advantageous Strategy*, Science, 1997 (275): 1293.

network of reasoning and constitute a part of the decision making process, instead of opposing it: feelings allow to operate advantageous choices, without having to produce advantageous assessments. Damasio suggests that during evolution, cognitive processes were added to feelings, maintaining the centrality of feelings in decision making. This hypothesis is supported by the fact that when in danger, when choices need to be done quickly, reasoning is bypassed and instantaneous decisions take place, in which the role of reasoning is limited.

The study of neurological patients affected by decision making deficits indicates that the processes which usually are judged necessary and sufficient for rational processes are intact. Tests show that short and long term memory, operational memory, attention, perception, language, abstract logic, arithmetical abilities, intelligence and learning, are working perfectly. Subjects respond in a normal way to cognitive tests and their functions are undamaged. They show normal intellect, but are unable to decide in an appropriate way for their future. A dissociation between the ability to decide advantageously and the ability to decide for objects, numbers and space is observed. In neuropsychology this deficit is described as dissociation between cognitive abilities and their use. On one side the cognitive abilities are undamaged, on the other side the patient is not able to use them advantageously for the future.

Decision making deficits are always accompanied by alterations in the ability to feel and this suggests that during evolution the strategies of reasoning have been guided by biological mechanisms of which feelings are an important aspect. This hypothesis does not contradict the fact that emotions can cause disorders in the reasoning processes, but underlines the extraordinary fact that the absence of feelings can be even more damaging. While all the cognitive functions of patients with decision making deficits are intact, the ability to feel is visibly altered: antisocial behaviour, behaviour against ethics and cold reasoning can be observed. These patients are always neutral, with no sadness, no impatience or frustration. They show the absence of feelings, positive or negative.

Furthermore, subjects affected by decision making deficit behave as *"short sighted toward the future."* This same deficit affects those who are under the effect of alcohol or drugs. The absence of feelings leads to the inability to feel the future and choose advantageously, the inability to plan the future also for the coming hours, confusion about priorities, the absence of intuitions and the absence of any trace of precognition.

On the contrary subjects who put forward advantageous strategies rely on feelings which:

1. help to orient rationality in the correct direction;
2. lead to the appropriate decisions in which it is possible to use correctly the instruments of logic;
3. help to forecast an uncertain future;
4. help in organizing actions, activate experiences of precognitions;
5. favor ethical judgments;

6. favor the harmonization of individual behaviour with social conventions.

Decision making deficit is often associated to specific lesions of the prefrontal cortex (PFC), especially in those sectors which integrate signals arriving from the body and which lead to the absence or the imperfect perception of feelings. People with these lesions are characterized by knowing but not by feeling. Prefrontal cortex lesions impair feelings and patients lose the ability to choose advantageously even if mental abilities are intact. Feelings involved in decision making are heart feelings, in the form of accelerated heartbeat, lungs feelings, in the form of contraction of breath and gut feelings.

In patients with prefrontal leucotomy extreme anxiety vanishes, but also their ability to feel vanishes. These patients become calm, they don't suffer any longer, but their ability to decide and to act is compromised.

Decision making deficits suggest that goal oriented systems, moved by finalities are based on feelings. These systems use feelings and body signals from the heart, lungs, intestine and muscles.

Between the "low" old brain structure involved in biological regulations and the "high" new structures involved in rational processes and thinking there is a great difference. Generally it is believed that they have different roles. At the higher levels will and reasoning occur, while at the lower levels feelings take place. Decision making deficits suggest that rationality and will do not take place without feelings. It seems that nature has built the cortical structures not just over the subcortical ones, but based on them.

Deciding well also means deciding quickly, especially when the time factor is essential, or at least deciding within a time lapse which is adequate to the problem. Calculating costs and benefits is slow and often inconclusive, because it requires to keep track of all the possibilities.

The cold strategy of rationality describes the way in which patients affected by prefrontal damages behave in order to decide, and not the way in which normal subjects behave when they have to take a decision.

Damasio recalls the words of Blaise Pascal: *"We think very little of time present; we anticipate the future"* and *"the heart has its reasons which reason knows nothing of."*

Pascal underlines the virtual inexistence of the present: the decision making process is always oriented to the future. Reasoning and decision making are an all-inclusive process of anticipation and creation of the future. We need some kind of strategy which produces reliable inferences about the future, on which to base an adequate response and which can support reasoning.

When talking about decision making the reference is usually to rationality and rarely to feelings. Damasio suggests that feelings transform decision making into a much faster, efficient and precise process and describes intuition as that mysterious process through which feelings lead us to the solution of a problem without thinking about it. He recalls the words of the mathematician Henri Poincaré.[21] Poincaré

---

[21] Henri Poincaré, *Mathematical Creation, from Science et méthode*, 1908.

shows that it is not necessary to apply reasoning to all the possible options, because some kind of pre-selection takes place. Some type of mechanism operates this selection, and allows only a limited number of possibilities to reach the conscious mind. These possibilities arise top the conscious mind thanks to feelings of certainty.

According to Leo Szilard: *"Scientists have a lot in common with artists and poets. Logic and analytical thinking are necessary attributes of the scientist, but are not sufficient for a creative work. In science intuitions which have led to progress are not logically derived from pre-existing knowledge: creative processes on which the progress of science is based operate at an unconscious level."*[22]

In the perspective of evolution it seems that the autonomic nervous system is the way by which the brain of simple organisms regulates the internal functions of the body.

The autonomic nervous system, also known as visceral nervous system, is the part of the peripheral nervous system that acts as a control system functioning largely below the level of consciousness. It affects heart rate, digestion, respiration rate, salivation, perspiration, diameter of the pupils and sexual arousal. Whereas most of its actions are involuntary, some, such as breathing, work in tandem with the conscious mind.

The autonomic nervous system is divided into two sub-systems, the parasympathetic and sympathetic systems, one sensory and afferent, the other motor and efferent. Within

---

[22] Szilard L (1992), in Lanouette W, *Genius in the Shadows, Charles Scribner's Sons*, New York 1992.

these systems there are inhibitory and excitatory synapses. Classical measurements of the autonomic nervous system parameters are: heart rate frequency, skin conductance and body temperature.

- Experiments with guessing tasks

Bechara, a student following a specialization course in Damasio's laboratory, devised a guessing task which is different from other similar experiments.[23] Patients and normal subjects enjoyed a setting in which real life situations took place, far away from the artificial setting of typical neurophysiological tasks. Bechara wanted to be as "realistic" as possible in order to assess the decision making capabilities in a natural setting.

In the main experiment the subject is seated in front of a table on which 4 decks of cards are placed, each marked with a different letter: A, B, C and D. Subjects receive 2,000 dollars (false, but perfectly resembling true money) and are told that the aim of the game is to lose the least and try to win as much as possible. The game consists in uncovering cards, one at a time, from any of the decks, until the experimenter stops the game. Each card is associated with a gain or a loss of money. Only when a card is turned it is possible to know how much the subject has earned or lost. At the beginning subjects have no way to predict what is

---

[23] Bechara A (2005), Damasio H, Tranel D and Damasio AR, *The Iowa Gambling Task and the somatic marker hypothesis: some questions and answers*, Trends in Cognitive Sciences, 9: 4, April 2005.

going to happen and are not able to keep in mind the sequence of gains and losses. The game takes place, as in real life, where knowledge arrives slowly, while experience increases.

It is interesting to observe how subjects behave during the experiments. They start testing each of the decks, searching cues and regularities. Then, maybe attracted by the high gains, they show a first preference for the decks A and B which lead to higher gains but also to much higher losses, then after the first 30 cards they change strategy and start choosing decks C and D until the end of the game. Some players, who declare they like to risk occasionally go back to decks A and B, but only in order to move back to decks C and D.

Players do not have a way to perform a precise calculation of gains and losses, but gradually develop the knowledge that decks A and B are more dangerous.

The behaviour of patients with frontal lesions was opposite from that of normal subjects. Patients with frontal damages, even if cooperative and paying a lot of attention to the game, chose in a disastrous way.

A lot is known about the neural networks in the damaged areas, but why does the damage of this areas block any perception of what the future consequences of choices could be?

Both normal subjects and patients with frontal damages produce skin conductance reactions each time they receive a gain or a loss after they turn a card. In other words, immediately after the gain or the loss subjects show, through skin conductance reactions, that they have been influenced by the outcome.

However in normal subjects, after they have turned a certain number of cards, something different happens. Just before they choose a card from a dangerous deck, that is to say when they have decided to choose from a risky deck, a skin conductance response is observed which increases while the game progresses. Damasio interprets this result saying that the brain learns gradually the possible negative outcome of each deck, and before a card is chosen it informs the subject through the activation of a somatic marker, which in this case can be measured using skin conductance.

The fact that subjects with neuronal damages did not show this arousal of skin conductance proves, according to Damasio, that this activation is acquired through experience, and that it increases during the experiment, and that this somatic marker tries to inform the subject about a future outcome which could be positive or negative.

Patients with frontal injuries, on the contrary, do not show this anticipatory reaction of skin conductance, they do not show signs that their brain is learning to predict the negative outcome.

Damasio says that it is still unknown how the experiment with the cards leads to predict future outcomes. It might be that the subject develops a cognitive strategy of negative and positive outcomes and connects automatically this impression with a somatic marker which informs about the future negative outcome which then operates as an alarm signal. In this model reasoning (a cognitive guess) precedes the somatic marker; but this is the critical point as neurological patients cannot operate "normal" decisions even though they know which are the good and bad decks. A second model says that the somatic marker precedes reasoning. According to this model biological processes would pave the way to a rational and conscious decision. When this biological process of information does not take place, it would be difficult to arrive at the end of the decision making because it would require too much time.

Damasio does not want to say that mind is in the body, but he states that the role of the body is not limited to the modulation of vital functions, since it also includes information, in the way of feelings which are vital for the normal functioning of reasoning.

The somatic marker hypothesis posits that feelings mark relevant information about the future outcome of an event. Feelings produce these markers in a totally manifest way, in the form of visceral feeling, heart feelings, but also using signals which cannot be consciously perceived by the brain.

In conclusion, Bechara and Damasio observes 3 types of activation of skin conductance:

1. Two activations "after", one after the positive outcome and one after the negative outcome.
2. One activation "before" the choice of a negative deck.

Damasio interprets this last anticipatory reaction of the skin conductance as an effect of learning.

RETROCAUSALITY OR LEARNING?

The fourth experiment uses the same sequence of colors as the first experiment, but in the third phase one color has a 35% chance of being selected by the computer (lucky color), one has a 15% chance (unlucky color) and the last two colors have a 25% chance (neutral colors). The task given to the subjects is to guess the highest number of colors selected by the computer (target). Subjects are not aware that colors have a different chance of being selected.

This design allows to study together Fantappiè's retrocausal hypothesis, Damasio's learning hypothesis and their interaction:

1. *Retrocausal effect.* Differences in heart rate (HR) frequencies observed in phase 1, in association with unpredictable random targets selected by the computer in phase 3 can be attributed only to a retrocausal effect.
2. *Learning effect.* Differences in heart rate (HR) frequencies observed in phase 1, in association with the choice operated by the subject in phase 2, can be interpreted as a learning effect.

Hypotheses are the following:

1. *Retrocausal hypothesis:* differences in heart rate (HR) measurements in phase 1 are expected in association

with target colors (phase 3). These differences will be interpreted as retrocausal effects, considering the fact that the selection of target colors happens in phase 3 and heart rates are measured in phase 1.

2. *Learning hypothesis*: according to the works of Damasio and Bechara a learning effect is expected in the form of heart rate differences measured in phase 1 in association with the choice (lucky and unlucky) operated by the subject in phase 2; these differences should increase during the experiment.

3. *Interaction between retrocausal and learning effect*: the retrocausal effect and the learning effect share the same somatic markers and are therefore both assessed through heart rates. The hypothesis is that at the beginning of the experiment only the retrocausal effect can be detected, then the learning effect starts building up and disturbs the retrocausal effect which decreases. At the end the retrocausal and learning effects separate and can be detected. Clues of a possible interaction emerged during the development of the software. Subjects involved in the first 3 experiments reported a "butterfly" feeling in the stomach in association with the choice of target stimuli, whereas subjects involved in testing the design of this last experiment did not report the butterfly feeling and the retrocausal effect showed with less strength. This fact suggested that the learning effect could disturb the retrocausal effect.

From a software perspective the different probability for

each color was obtained randomly selecting in phase 3 a number from 1 to 100. When the number was between 1 and 35 the lucky color was shown, between 36 and 50 the unlucky color was shown, between 51 and 75 the first neutral color was shown and between 76 and 100 the last neutral color was shown.

The same number could be selected again, making each number totally independent from the previous ones. In the 3,000 trials of this experiment (30 subjects x 100 trials per subject) the lucky color was selected 36.15% times, the unlucky color 14.13% and the neutral colors 24.86% each.

The experiment was conducted in the period March/April 2009, the following instructions were given to the experimenter: inform the subject about the total time of the experiment (around 40 minutes); choose a quiet room, where the subject can be left alone for all the length of the experiment; start the recording of the heart rate frequency only after it has stabilized (initially, heart rate frequency measurements are altered because of the movements that the subject makes in order to apply the heart rate measuring device; the stabilization of the heart rate requires less than a minute from when the subject sits in front of the computer); inform the subject about the task (try to guess the highest number of colors selected by the computer); begin the experiment only after starting the recording of the heart rate measurements; follow the subject for the first trial, in order to check that he has understood the task; leave the subject alone in the room where the experiment is carried out.

At the end of each experiment the following 2 files were merged:

1. the file with heart rate measurements, produced by the SUUNTO software Training Monitor 2.2.0. In this file heart rate measurements are associated with the time of the measurement;

2. the file produced by the software developed in Delphi Pascal for the execution of the experiment. This file contains the exact time of presentation of stimuli (in milliseconds), the choice operated by the subject and the selection operated by the computer, associated with the characteristics of the stimuli.

For each subject an immediate feedback of the retrocausal effect was provided in the form of a table which briefly showed the observed differences:

Example of feed-back table								
Subject n. 21					Subject n. 7			
	Blue	Green	Red	Yellow		Blue	Green	Red	Yellow
HR 1:	-0.671	2.200	-0.840	-1.103	HR 1:	0.276	-0.775	0.040	0.378
HR 2:	-0.772	2.399	-0.556	-1.471	HR 2:	0.231	-0.750	0.133	0.298
HR 3:	-0.950	2.467	-0.056	-1.766	HR 3:	0.210	-0.862	0.173	0.414
HR 4:	-1.353	2.310	1.080	-2.054	HR 4:	0.150	-0.913	0.187	0.560
HR 5:	-1.928	2.204	1.894	-1.892	HR 5:	0.117	-0.850	0.187	0.545
HR 6:	-1.954	1.897	2.474	-1.993	HR 6:	0.048	-0.875	0.227	0.640
HR 7:	-1.982	1.535	2.752	-1.755	HR 7:	-0.067	-0.688	0.320	0.491
HR 8:	-2.015	1.543	2.733	-1.704	HR 8:	-0.077	-0.763	0.373	0.524
HR 9:	-1.831	1.397	2.665	-1.704	HR 9:	-0.129	-0.712	0.427	0.482
HR 10:	-1.770	1.508	2.407	-1.691	HR 10:	-0.109	-0.700	0.467	0.375
HR 11:	-1.482	1.468	1.981	-1.641	HR 11:	-0.174	-0.625	0.467	0.402
HR 12:	-1.458	1.853	1.404	-1.637	HR 12:	-0.249	-0.650	0.600	0.378
HR 13:	-1.572	2.154	1.199	-1.679	HR 13:	-0.259	-0.625	0.573	0.402
HR 14:	-1.544	2.079	1.260	-1.676	HR 14:	-0.296	-0.525	0.573	0.348
HR 15:	-1.452	1.994	1.226	-1.661	HR 15:	-0.283	-0.513	0.507	0.405
HR 16:	-1.311	1.727	1.255	-1.541	HR 16:	-0.220	-0.525	0.413	0.438
General total:	83.764				General total:	0.000			

In the previous example we see tables for subjects n. 21 and n. 7. Feedback tables consisted of 16 lines, one for each of the 16 heart rate frequencies measured in phase 1. Phase 1 is repeated 100 times. It is therefore possible to calculate 16 mean value differences for each color when it is target and when it is not target. These differences provide a feedback about the retrocausal effect.

For subject n. 21, in the first line (HR 1), we read that the mean value difference of the heart rate frequencies in phase 1, when the target is blue compared to when the blue is not a target is 0,671 heart beats lower. The second line is relative to the second heart rate frequency measured in phase 1 and its value for the blue color, when target, is 0,772 heart beats per minute lower.

The greater the difference between mean values (both positive and negative), the greater is the retrocausal effect. Statistical analyses were performed considering only differences greater than 1.5, since these values usually indicate a 0.01 probability error. A general total value is calculated considering the absolute values (differences without sign) above the value 1.5. For subject 21 we get a general total effect of 83.764, whereas for subject 7 we have a general total effect equal to zero.

Feedback tables can be represented graphically. We see that the retrocausal effect spreads all over phase 1. It is important to note that the effect is not limited to when the target color is shown in phase 1. In the first three experiments only heart rates measurements in association to the presentation of the target color in phase 1 were considered in the statistical data analyses.

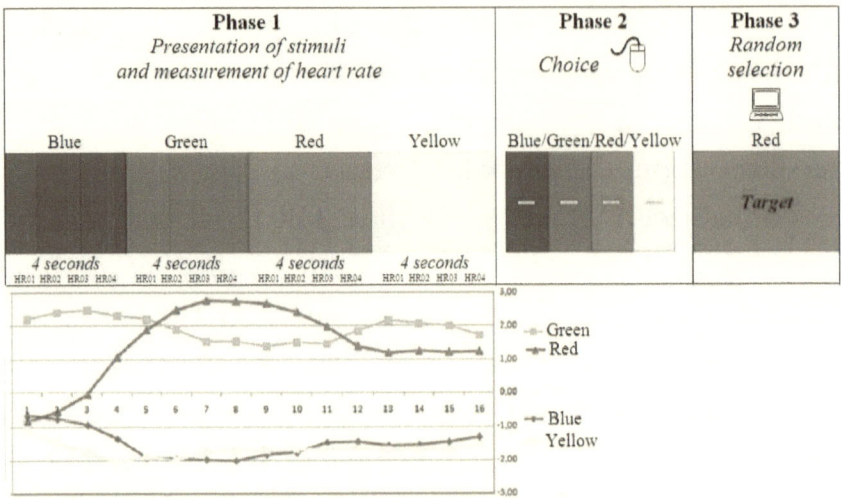

Feedback tables were used to assess if something was hindering the experiment. In the first 7 subjects the effect was practically null: 4 subjects showed a general total equal to zero and 3 showed a general value lower than 15. The experiment was being conducted using an old laptop computer with a low brightness of the display. It was decided to change computer with brighter colors and a wider screen. Once this change was made, a sudden increase in the values of the effect in the feedback tables was observed. Using the new computer sixteen subjects showed general values of the effect over 15, three lower than 15 and five equal to zero. Changing computer the number of subjects with no effect decreased from 57% to 21%.

When the total value in the feedback tables is calculated adding the real values (with the sign) it tends to zero. This explains why the differences, comparing all targets and non-targets in the first experiment, were null, whereas when the comparison was made within each color they became statistically meaningful.

The fact that the direction of the effect can diverge and that when added together it produces a null effect, points to the inadequateness of parametric statistics. In this last experiment, data analysis was carried out using nonparametric statistical techniques, based on frequency distributions and using the Chi Square and exact test of Fisher.

Mean values in feedback tables became the raw data. Trials were divided into 3 groups: the first 33 trials (starting from the second trial) the central 33 trials and the last 33 trials. For each subject 3 feedback tables were used. The first trial was removed from the tables. Consequently, data analyses considered 99 trials: from the 2nd to the 100th trial.

The *learning effect* was analyzed using "choice feedback tables". Choice feedback tables were calculated for each subject, for each group of trial (first 33 trials, central 33 trials and last 33 trials) and were relative to each of the 16 HR measured in phase 1. Differences of HR values were calculated in association with the choice (lucky, unlucky and neutral) operated by the subject in phase 2.

In the following example a "choice feedback table" is shown for subject n. 20.

Differences in heart rate mean values measured in phase 1 in association with the choice operated by the subject in phase 2							
Subject 20 – first 33 trials				Subject 20 – last 33 trials			
Choice:	Neutral	Lucky	Unlucky	Choice:	Neutral	Lucky	Unlucky
HR 1:	-1.857	1.597	0.800	HR 1:	-0.202	3.143	-1.591
HR 2:	-1.790	1.472	0.845	HR 2:	1.136	2.507	-2.727
HR 3:	-1.070	0.722	0.675	HR 3:	1.283	2.300	-2.773
HR 4:	-0.412	0.167	0.380	HR 4:	1.577	2.121	-3.000
HR 5:	-0.055	0.181	-0.120	HR 5:	1.375	1.729	-2.545
HR 6:	0.283	0.306	-0.715	HR 6:	1.515	0.907	-2.227
HR 7:	0.577	0.056	-0.845	HR 7:	1.768	0.414	-2.227
HR 8:	0.706	0.194	-1.170	HR 8:	1.783	-0.479	-1.727
HR 9:	0.044	1.139	-1.290	HR 9:	1.669	-0.807	-1.409
HR 10:	-0.673	1.194	-0.375	HR 10:	1.915	-1.443	-1.318
HR 11:	-1.033	0.958	0.370	HR 11:	2.353	-2.136	-1.409
HR 12:	-0.912	0.500	0.700	HR 12:	2.599	-3.243	-1.045
HR 13:	-0.790	0.042	1.030	HR 13:	3.206	-3.714	-1.455
HR 14:	-0.614	-0.139	0.985	HR 14:	3.801	-4.871	-1.455
HR 15:	-0.070	-0.403	0.530	HR 15:	3.423	-4.921	-1.000
HR 16:	0.713	-0.736	-0.175	HR 16:	2.941	-4.143	-0.909
General total:	5.244			General total:	128.018		

Values tending to zero indicate no anticipatory heart rate reaction previous to the choice, whereas high values (positive or negative) indicate an anticipatory reaction. Choice tables data were represented graphically in the following way:

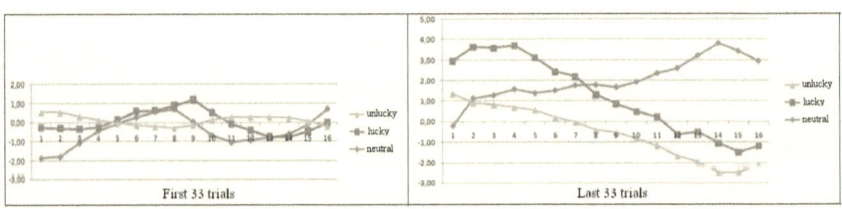

Graphical representation of the choice feedback table for subject n. 20

In this graphical representation we see in the last 33 trials a sharp increase in the anticipatory effect, as it is expected by Damasio's learning hypothesis.

Dividing choice and feedback tables in 3 groups (first 33 trials, central 33 trials and last 33 trials), the cut off value of

1.5 does not correspond any longer to a probability error of 1% (p<0.01), but it was considered a good threshold value for the analyses.

In order to calculate Chi Square values, expected frequencies were needed. These were obtained "empirically" using non correlated targets (NCT): targets which are not correlated with the selection operated by the computer in phase 3.

NCT can be generated using loops, in which the first target is blue, the second green, the third red and the fourth yellow and repeating this sequence for all the 100 trials. It was decided to use loops, since targets generated randomly produce expected frequency distributions which vary and which require the experimenter to choose among distributions. This could lead to an artifact since a distribution which is most convenient in order to obtain statistically significant results could be chosen.

Using NCT for the production of expected frequencies, the following table was obtained for the retrocausal effect:

Frequencies	Differences of the mean values			Total
	Up to -1.500	-1.499 to +1.499	+1.500 and over	
Observed	1053 (17.83%)	3680 (63.89%)	1027 (18.28%)	5760 (100%)
Expected	781 (13.56%)	4225 (73.35%)	754 (13.09%)	5760 (100%)

Observed and expected frequencies in the distribution of mean differences of HR, measured in phase 1 in association with target colors selected by the computer in phase 3. Chi Square = 263.86.
Value of Chi Square 13.81 corresponds to p=0.001

Representing this table in a graphical way:

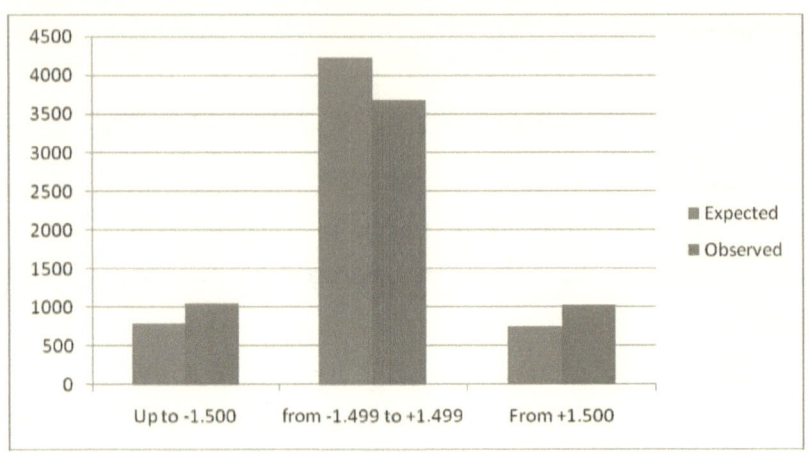

Graphical representation of the retrocausal effect

In the first group, on the left, differences up to -1.5 are associated with an observed frequency of 17.83% and an expected frequency of 13.56%; in the central class (from -1.499 to +1.499) the observed frequency is 63.89% compared to an expected frequency of 73.35%; in the last class, on the right, the observed frequency is 18.28%, the expected frequency is 13.09%.

The difference between observed and expected frequencies is equal to a Chi Square of 263.86 which, compared to 13.81 for an error probability of $p<0.001$, results to be extremely significant. It was not possible to use the exact test of Fisher since this test can be applied only to 2x2 tables.

In first three experiments the retrocausal effect could be seen only on some colors which changed randomly from one experiment to the other. This was caused by parametric statistics. When the analysis is carried out using nonparametric statistics, where the effect does not need to be added, it shows on all the colors:

Differences	Colours				Total	N.C.T.
	Blue	Green	Red	Yellow		
From + 1.500	14.0%	22.0%	19.6%	15.7%	17.8%	13.09%
-1.499 to +1.499	60.7%	64.9%	64.6%	65.3%	63.9%	73.35%
Up to -1.500	25.3%	13.1%	15.8%	19.0%	18.3%	13.56%
	100%	100%	100%	100%	100%	100.00%
	(n=1,440)	(n=1,440)	(n=1,440)	(n=1,440)	(n=5,760)	

Distribution of the differences of HR mean values (phase 1) associated with the selection operated by the computer (phase 3).

The Chi Square value for the blue color is 176.41 equivalent to $p<1/10^{27}$, for the green color the retrocausal effect is Chi Square 102.7, for the red color 60.82 and for the yellow color 56.67. A graphical representation of these results is the following:

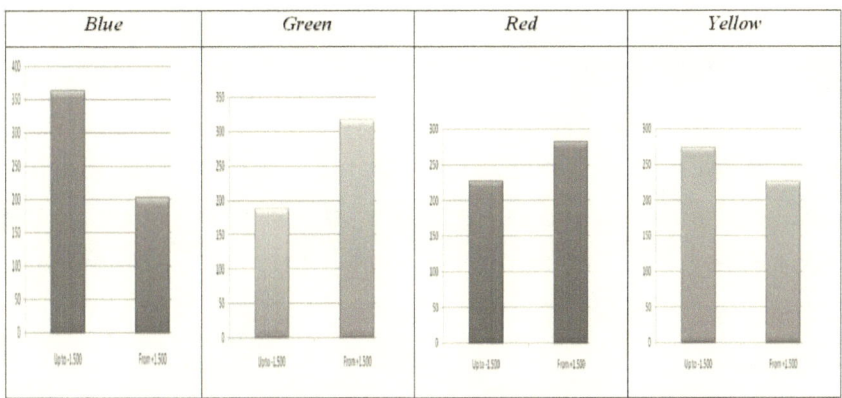

Positive and negative statistically significant differences of HR per color.
Whilst on the blue color the effect prevalently takes the form of a decrease in HR and on the green color it takes the form of an increase in the HR, for red and yellow the effect is distributed in a balanced way between subjects who show a significant increase in HR and subjects who show a significant decrease in HR, becoming therefore invisible to parametric statistical analyses.

This graphical representation shows that for the blue and green colors the retrocausal effect is unbalanced. This unbalanced distribution of the positive and negative side of the effect permits to see the effect also when using parametric statistics. In the case of the red and yellow colors, the negative side and positive side of the effect are balanced and therefore they become invisible to parametric statistics.

Fisher's exact test requires 2x2 tables where only one cell is compared with all the rest. The difference between observed and expected frequencies for the blue color corresponds to a statistically significant value of $p=0,4/10^{14}$, that is to say an error probability of $p=0.000000000000004$. This value has been calculated without using the non-correlated targets (NCT), but using only the totals of the 2x2 tables, and it still confirms the retrocausal effect.

Damasio's learning hypothesis states that the choice (guess) of the subject in phase 2 is preceded by the activation of neurophysiological parameters of the autonomic nervous system such as skin conductance and heart rate frequencies. The learning hypothesis expects a stronger activation of the heart rate frequency in the last trials of the experiment.

Differences	Colour chosen by the subject			Total	N.C.T.
	Neutral	Lucky	Unlucky		
From + 1.500	14.0%	16.6%	17.2%	16.0%	13.1%
- 1,499 to +1,499	73.5%	66.0%	66.0%	68.5%	73.3%
Up to -1,500	12.5%	17.4%	16.8%	15.5%	13.6%
	100%	100%	100%	100%	100.0%
	(n=1,440)	(n=1,440)	(n=1,440)	(n=4,320)	

Global learning effect.
Distribution of HR differences (phase 1) in association with the color chosen by the subject in phase 2. This table was calculated considering all the subjects and all the trials.

The observed frequencies for neutral colors coincide with the expected frequencies (73.5% compared to 73.3 expected), whereas for the lucky and unlucky colors there is a difference between observed frequencies and expected ones. This difference is associated with a Chi Square of 39.15 ($p<1/10^9$) which shows a learning effect.

The subject can choose among four colors: two neutral colors, a lucky color and an unlucky color. At the start of the experiment participants were told that colors are random. During the experiment the subject should learn the different probabilities and this would show in the form of a different activation of heart rate frequencies in phase 1, before operating the choice in phase 2.

Lucky, unlucky and neutral colors are selected randomly at the start of the experiment. During the execution of the experiment no one knows which are the lucky and unlucky colors, only at the end of the experiment this information is saved in the data file. The hypothesis is that the learning effect should increase while the experiment progresses and that it should be particularly strong in the last trials.

Differences	Trial			Total	N.C.T.
(absolute values)	2-34	35-67	68-100		
Up to 1.499	69.4%	73.8%	62.3%	68.5%	73.3%
From 1.500	30.6%	26.2%	37.7%	31.5%	26.7%
	100%	100%	100%	100%	100.0%
	(n=1,440)	(n=1,440)	(n=1,440)	(n=4,320)	

Distribution of mean differences of HR measured in phase 1 according to the choice operated by the subject in phase 2, divided for group of trials.

The previous table shows an initial effect in the first 33 trials with a Chi Square value of 11,53, just over 0.001 of probability. In the middle 33 trials no effect is observed. In the last 33 trials the distribution differs significantly from the expected one (N.C.T. column). Chi Square value is 89,77 which corresponds to $p<1/10^{22}$. These results show that in the last 33 trials of the experiment the learning effect is strongly significant.

The following table considers only the last 33 trials. In this table the learning effect of the lucky and unlucky colors is stronger, compared to the general table.

Differences	Colour chosen by the subject			Total	N.C.T.
	Neutral	Lucky	Unlucky		
From + 1.500	15.8%	19.2%	24.0%	19.6%	13.1%
- 1.499 to +1.499	68.4%	57.7%	60.8%	62.3%	73.3%
Up to -1.500	15.8%	23.1%	15.2%	18.1%	13.6%
	100% (n=480)	100% (n=480)	100% (n=480)	100% (n=1.440)	100.0%

Distribution of the differences among mean HR values measured in phase 1 associated with the choice performed by the subject (phase 2). This table is relative to the last group of 33 trials, for all the subjects.

We see that the effect does not always show in the same direction and it is therefore not additive.

Differences (absolute values)	Trial			Total	N.C.T.
	2-34	35-67	68-100		
Up to 1.499	59.6%	70.8%	61.2%	63.9%	73,3%
From 1.500	40.4%	29.2%	38.8%	36.1%	26,7%
	100% (n=1,920)	100% (n=1,920)	100% (n=1,920)	100% (n=5,760)	100,0%

Distribution of mean value HR differences in phase 1 associated with the target selected by the computer in phase 3

In this last table, which is relative to the retrocausal effect, we see that the effect is strong in the first 33 trials, it becomes null in the middle trials and it becomes again strong in the last 33 trials. Using the exact test of Fisher, in the first 33 trials the effect is strongly significant with $p < 0.76/10^{13}$, in the middle trials it practically disappears, but in the last 33 trials it turns out again to be strongly significant with $p = 0.95/10^{10}$.

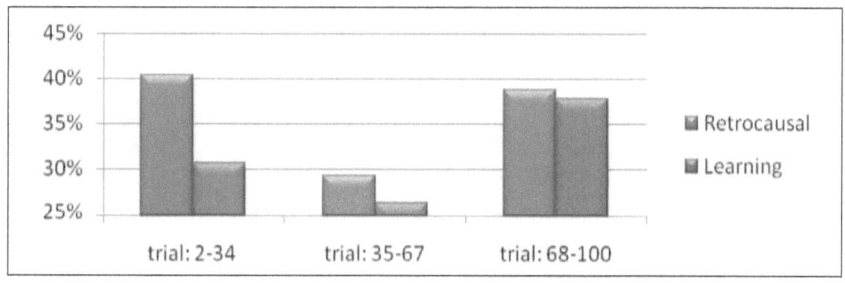

Interaction between retrocausal and learning effect.
Statistical significance of 1% starts at frequency values of 29%

Considering together the retrocausal and learning effect we see a strong retrocausal effect in the first 33 trials, whereas the learning effect is limited. Then, in the middle trials both the learning and retrocausal effect disappear. At the end of the experiment, in the last 33 trials, both effects become strongly significant. The increase in the last 33 trials coincides with $p = 0,95/10^{10}$ for the retrocausal effect and $p < 1/10^{22}$ for the learning effect.

In the first 33 trials the retrocausal effect is strong, since the learning effect has not yet emerged. The two effects conflict in the middle 33 trials causing a decrease of the retrocausal effect and in the last 33 trials a strong rise in both the effects is observed.

The next table is relative to the subject with the highest values of general differences in the feedback table. The retrocausal effect is extremely strong from the beginning of the experiment, but it drastically drops in the central part of the experiment where percentage values become similar to the expected ones (NCT column) and then becomes strong again in the last trials.

Differences (absolute values)	Trial			Total	N.C.T.
	2-34	35-67	68-100		
Up to 1.499	26.6%	67.2%	29.7%	44.0%	73.3%
From 1.500	73.4%	32.8%	70.3%	56.0%	26.7%
	100%	100%	100%	100%	100.0%
	(n=64)	(n=64)	(n=64)	(n=192)	

Distribution of mean differences of HR measured in phase 1 in association with the target selected by the computer in phase 3, divided by trials. This table considers only the data of the subject with the highest general total in the feedback table.

When subjects discover the existence of a lucky color he/she could start choosing always this color, increasing in this way the correct guesses from 25% (random) to 35% of the lucky color. This increase was not observed, in the first 33 trial the target was guessed correctly 24.75% times, in the middle trials 24.65% and in the last trials 25.47%. This data shows that even if the learning effect is strongly visible in HR differences, it does not enter the cognitive system.

METHODOLOGY OF CONCOMITANCES

In the experiments we have seen that when data analysis is conducted in a classical way, adding the effects among subjects, opposite effects cancel. This suggests that when studying retrocausality parametric statistical techniques are not suitable and the methodology of concomitant variations needs to be used.

Stuart Mill showed that relations can be studied using the methodology of differences and the methodology of concomitant variations.[24]

1. The <u>methodology of differences</u>: *"If an element of difference is introduced in two initially similar groups, the differences that are observed can only be attributed to this single element that was introduced."*
2. The <u>methodology of concomitant variations</u>: *"When two phenomena vary concomitantly, one may be the cause of the other or both are united by the same cause."*

When studying relations different from classical causality the methodology of concomitant variations is needed and this is always coupled with nonparametric statistics.

However science has been mainly using the experimental method based on the *methodology of differences*.

The methodology of differences works as follows:

---

[24] Stuart Mill, *A System of Logic*, 1843.

1. two similar groups are formed (they are named the experimental and the control group).
2. Treatment (the cause) is given only to the experimental group and all the other conditions are kept equal, so that the control group differs from the experimental group only for the treatment.
3. Consequently, any difference observed between the experimental group and the control group can be attributed solely to the treatment, because only this condition changes between the two groups.

In order to have similar groups, randomization is used in the belief that it should distribute evenly all the intervening variables, between the experimental and the control group. But, generally speaking, no controls are performed in order to verify if the condition of similarity is satisfied and often the experimental and control groups are different ever since the beginning of the experiment. A single subject with extreme values can produce differences which are not due to the cause (ie treatment), but are due to the initial dissimilarity of the control and experimental groups.

In order to test the effect of a drug the experimental procedure is the following:

1. two similar groups are formed, assigning subjects randomly to the experimental group or to the control group.
2. The drug is given only to the experimental group, while

all the other circumstances are left similar. The control group is therefore given a placebo, a similar substance which has no effect.

3. The differences observed between the two groups can be attributed solely to the effect of the drug.

Differences are the effect and the drug (also called treatment) is the cause. The following conditions are required:

1. In order to study differences between groups it is necessary that the effect can be _added_ among the experimental subjects. For example, if a drug increases in some subjects the reaction times, whereas in others subjects it reduces the reaction times, when adding these opposite effects a null effect is obtained. The effect exists, but it is invisible to the experimental methodology based on the study of differences.

2. Differences can be calculated only when using _quantitative data_ (ie data which can be added together). On the contrary, qualitative data cannot be added and it is unsuitable when using the experimental method.

3. All possible _sources of variability must be controlled_. It is important that nothing, besides the treatment (ie the cause), can influence the variability of groups. For this reason a controlled environment, which allows to keep alike all the possible sources of variability and in which each subject is treated exactly in the same way, is needed. Controlled environments require laboratory settings,

which are very different from the natural context. The need for controlled settings limits the experimental method to analytical knowledge, detached from the context and from complexity.

4. It is possible to study differences considering only one cause at a time or at the most few causes when studying their interaction.

5. When samples are small (less than 300 subjects), randomization does not guarantee the similarity of groups, and differences between groups may not depend on the treatment, but on the initial diversity of groups.

Common mistakes:

1. Differences can be caused by single extreme values. Just one single outlier[25] can cause statistical significant results and lead to assert effects that do not exist. Outliers are often kept or removed in order to manipulate results.

2. In statistics, data transformation refers to the application of a deterministic mathematical function to each point in a data set which is replaced with the transformed value. A common example are logarithmic transformations. In theory, any mathematical function can be used to transform the data set. Operating in this way, it is often possible to obtain differences between the two data sets, when there are no effects.

3. When the effect shows in opposite directions, differences cannot be assessed and the effect becomes

---

[25] In statistics, an outlier is an observation that is distant from other observations.

invisible.

From a statistical point of view the methodology of differences uses parametric statistical techniques which compare mean and variance values, such as Student's t and the analysis of variance (ANOVA). These techniques require that effects can be added, that data is quantitative and normally distributed (according to a Gaussian distribution), and groups are initially similar and are from the same population. But, these requirements cannot be met in life sciences and parametric techniques end producing results that are inconsistent.

It is therefore of no surprise that a study published on JAMA (Journal of the American Medical Association), which revisited the results produced using the experimental method (ANOVA) and published in the period from 1990 to 2003 in 3 major scientific journals and cited at least 1,000 times, found that a study out of three was refuted by other experimental works. This finding raises serious doubts about the experimental method, when used in life sciences.[26]

In May 2011 Arrosmith published in the Journal Nature a study which shows that the ability to reproduce the results from phase 1 to phase 2 decreased in the period 2008-2010 from 28% to 18%, despite results were statistically robust in phase 1 (phase 1 indicates studies conducted on small groups, generally not exceeding 100 subjects, whereas phase 2 indicates studies conducted on larger groups, usually not

---

[26] Ioannidis J.P.A. (2005), *Contradicted and Initially Stronger Effects in Highly Cited Clinical Research*, JAMA 2005; 294: 218-228.

exceeding 300 subjects).[27]

Gautam Naik in the article "*Scientists' Elusive Goal: Reproducing Study Results*" published on the Wall Street Journal on December 2, 2011 points out that one of the secrets of medical research is that the majority of results, including those published in major scientific journals, cannot be reproduced.

Reproducibility is at the foundations of making science and when results are not reproduced the consequences can be devastating.[28] Naik notes that researchers, particularly in universities, need to find positive results in order to publish and receive funding.

In the December 23, 2010 article entitled "*The Truth Wears Off,*" published in The New Yorker, Jonah Lehrer quotes a passage of a letter from a university professor, now an employee of a biotechnology industry:

> "*When I worked in a university lab, we'd find all sorts of ways to get a significant result. We'd adjust the sample size after the fact, perhaps because some of the mice were outliers or maybe they were handled incorrectly, etc. This wasn't considered misconduct. It was just the way things were done. Of course, once these animals were thrown out [of the data] the effect of the intervention was publishable.*"

There is plenty of evidence that the massive financial

---

[27] Arrosmith J. (2011), *Trial watch: Phase II failures: 2008-2010*, Nature, May 2011, 328-329.
[28] Only in the US the biomedical industry invests each year more than 100 billion dollars in research

incentives lead to the suppression of negative results and the misinterpretation of positive ones. This helps explain, at least in part, why such a large percentage of randomized clinical trials cannot be replicated."

- The methodology of concomitant variations

In 1992 physicists at LEP (Large Electron-Positron Collider in operation at CERN in Geneva) could not explain some annoying fluctuations in the beams of electrons and positrons. Although very small, these fluctuations created serious problems when the energy of the rays must be measured with great precision. The experimental method did not provide any clue and in order to solve the dilemma the methodology of concomitant variations was used in order to test different hypotheses. Results showed the concomitant fluctuation in the energy of the particle beams of LEP and the tidal force exerted by the Moon. A more detailed analysis showed that the gravitational attraction of the Moon distorts very slightly the vast stretch of land where the circular tunnel of LEP is recessed. This tiny change in the size of the accelerator caused fluctuations of about 10 million electron volts in the energy rays.

The methodology of concomitant variations uses double entry tables of dichotomous variables.

For example:

	Males	Females	Total
No accidents	50	105	155
Accidents	200	45	245
Total	250	150	400

Concomitances between sex and car accidents
(data invented for this example)

In this table the concomitance of the variable sex and car accidents is difficult to assess, since the total values of each column differs. When the absolute frequency values are converted into column percentage values it becomes easy to compare the columns "Males" and "Females":

	Males	Females	Total
No accident	50	105	155
	20%	70%	39%
Accidents	200	45	245
	80%	30%	61%
Total	250	150	400
	100%	100%	100%

Concomitances between sex and car accidents
(columns percentages)

We now see a strong concomitance between "*Males*" and "*Accidents*" (80%) and between "*Females*" and "*No accidents*" (70%). Concomitances are assessed according to the differences between observed frequencies (column percentage) and expected frequencies (percentages in the total column). For example, the expected percentage for "*no accidents*" is 39%, whereas in the "*females*" column we have 70%.

Since being male is determined before accidents take place, we can fall in the error of stating that being male is the cause of car accidents. However, this methodology allows to study intervening variables by splitting the table in two. For example, we can split the previous table in two groups: those who drive little and those who drive a lot:

	Drive little		*Drive a lot*	
	Males	Females	Males	Females
No accidents	70%	70%	20%	20%
Accidents	30%	30%	80%	80%
Total	100%	100%	100%	100%

Concomitances between sex, km driven and car accidents

In this table the concomitances between sex and accidents disappears. The correlation *"males-accidents"* is therefore mediated by the variable *"number of kilometers driven"*, which is therefore an intervening variable. Consequently the relation becomes *"males drive a lot and consequently are involved in more accidents."* Crossing three variable at a time allows to identify intervening variables and to study the context within which relations are valid.

For example, when a concomitance is found between a drug and healing it is possible to study if it is true always, or only at certain conditions, such as specific age groups, sex, habits and other conditions.

The advantages of the methodology of concomitant variations are:

1. It uses dichotomous variables. Any information, quantitative or qualitative, objective or subjective can be transformed into one or more dichotomous variables. As a result it permits to keep track of all the elements of the phenomena.

2. It allows the study of many variables at the same time, thereby it can take into account the complexity of the phenomena. In contrast the experimental method can study only one or a limited number of variables at a time, thereby it produces knowledge which is detached from the context and the complexity of natural phenomena.

3. It allows to control for intervening and spurious variables, and this is done after and not before. Therefore, it does not always need controlled environments such as a laboratory and it is possible to use natural contexts.

4. With subjective answers people often respond using masks. For example, even when we feel unhappy, lonely, depressed, usually we try to give an image of ourselves (a mask) which is positive. With the experimental method masks constitute a problem which is insurmountable and which is solved only by removing qualitative and subjective information from the analyses. On the contrary, the methodology of concomitant variations can handle correctly responses which are masked.

This happens because a property of masks is that they affect not only one variable, but all those which are correlated. For example, if a person responds by saying no to "*I feel depressed*," when he is depressed, he will also say no to "*I feel unhappy*," when he is unhappy. The concomitance between depression and unhappiness remains unchanged, because both responses have moved in the same direction and continue to remain correlated.

	Depressed	Not Depressed	Total
Unhappy	15	3	18
Happy	2	*180*	182
Total	17	183	200

Concomitances between masked answers

This table shows that the two modalities, "*I feel happy*" and "*I do not feel depressed*", are concomitant.

When using psychological tests, which produce "objective" measurements of depression and happiness which are not distorted by the effect of masks, answers shift from the positive to the negative side. But the result remains unchanged:

	Depressed	Not Depressed	Total
Unhappy	*158*	10	168
Happy	2	30	32
Total	160	40	200

Concomitances obtained when using "objective" information

Results continue to show the concomitance between the

variables depression and unhappiness.

This means that if a concomitance exists it will show also when responses are masked, since masks are applied in a coherent way to all those variables which are correlated. This is a fundamental point, as the problem of masks is ubiquitous in psychological, social and economic sciences. The methodology of concomitant variations solves this problem and allows in this way to widen science to subjective and qualitative data and allows the methodology of concomitant variations to use direct questions, such as: *"do you feel depressed?"*

- Statistics

When using the methodology of concomitant variations, the first thing we have to do is to define which is the "statistical unit." Statistical units allow the study of concomitances among variables and the choice of the statistical unit is strictly related to the aim of the research. Units can be persons, animals, plants, manufactured items, organizations.

With the methodology of differences units are in a one-to-one correspondence with the data values, whereas with the methodology of concomitant variations there is a one-to-many correspondence, since unlimited data values can be collected for each unit.

Sample requirements differ according to the methodology and aim:

1. When the aim is to make inferences about the population from the sample, the sample must be representative of the population. This is usually achieved by random sampling.

2. When the aim is to study differences among the experimental and the control group the sample must be homogeneous. This is usually achieved by randomly distributing the units across the experimental and control group. If the aim is to assess the effect of a new drug against a placebo drug, then the patients should be allocated to either the drug group (experimental) or to the placebo group (control) using randomization. Randomization reduces biases by equally distributing factors that have not been explicitly accounted for. When randomization does not allow for the formation of homogeneous groups, the alternative is to use laboratory animals, purposely bred in order to guarantee homogeneity. Laboratory animals are euthanized after being used once, since their use in one experiment makes them different and unsuitable for other experiments.

3. When the aim is to study concomitant variations among variables, the sample must be heterogeneous. If the aim is to study which factors cause drug addiction, we will include in the sample subjects with different levels of drug addiction. The definition of the sample is therefore

strictly related to the aim. With the methodology of concomitant variations it is important to keep track of all the possible intervening variables, and check later for intervening and spurious relations.

The methodology of differences assesses effects by:

1. comparing the difference between mean values of the experimental and control groups with the variability of the values in the sample;
2. or by comparing the variance between groups with the variance within groups.

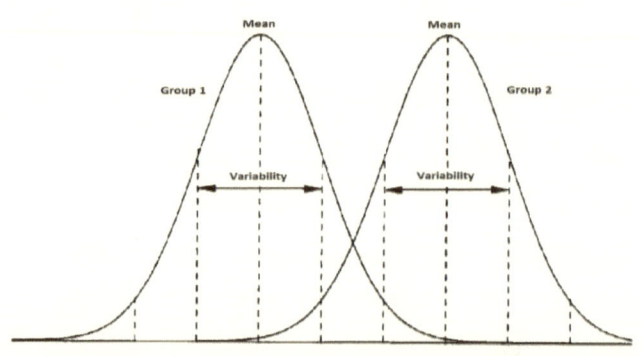

Comparison of mean and variability of two groups

Initial similarity between groups is a fundamental requirement, without which it is impossible to state that the difference observed between the experimental and the control group is a consequence of the cause/treatment. But, in clinical trials the variability of subjects can be so great that even increasing the sample size does not lead to statistical significant results.

When this is the case laboratory animals are used. Laboratory animals are all very similar and decrease the variability of the sample, allowing in this way small differences to become statistically significant.

There is now mounting evidence that animal experimentation constitutes an artifact.[29] The reason is very simple. Statistical significance is stronger when the variability is smaller. Consequently, when the effect size is small, the only way to obtain statistically significant results is to reduce the variability of the sample. When using animals, which are all very similar, the variability of the sample tends to be null, and consequently also insignificant differences become statistically significant. In other words, animals are too similar and differences that have no actual value become significant. Furthermore, one of the fundamental rules in science is to use samples that are representative of the population to which results will be generalized. It is obvious that laboratory animals are not representative of humans and that the effects observed using laboratory animals are difficult to generalize to humans.

Finally, the methodology of differences uses parametric statistical techniques, which require data distributed according to the Gaussian curve. This condition is usually not met, nevertheless researchers go on and interpret results.

---

[29] In experimental science, 'artifact' is used to refer to experimental results which are not manifestations of the natural phenomenon under investigation, but are due to the particular experimental arrangement, and hence indirectly to human agency.

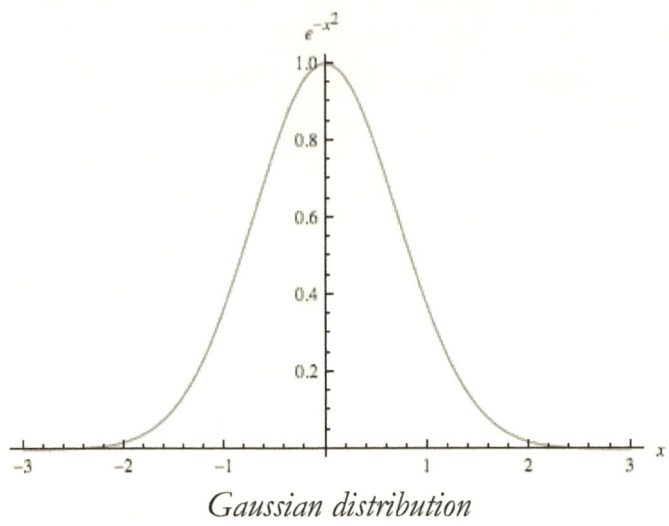

Gaussian distribution

Concomitances require variability: heterogeneous samples, where variability is maximized. The methodology of differences requires homogeneous samples, whereas the methodology of concomitant variations requires heterogeneous samples.

For example, with the methodology of concomitant variations, in a study that aims to compare the growth of 5 different types of crop in 5 different types of field, all the combinations will be considered (5! = 120 possible combinations) and at least 30 measurements will be taken for each combination. Since the aim is to compare growth rates, the statistical unit will be the height of the crop after a fixed interval of days (or a similar type of measurement). For each measurement an array of information will be traced, such as the type of field and the type of crop, secondly information that we think can be related to the growth of crop. At the end we will have 3600 records (30 measurement x 120 combinations), each with data on the growth rate and an array of other information.

When answers tend to concentrate in one modality, wider measuring scales are needed. For example, when we ask *"Do you feel depressed?"* yes/no, most people answer no and this little variability limits the possibility of studying concomitances. In order to restore variability it is necessary to use wider scales, such as *"How much do you feel depressed?"* *0,1,2,3,4,5,6,7,8,9,10*. Most answers will concentrate in the low values, 0 to 3, and the median cut-off point will probably be between the values 1 and 2. The aim of the methodology of concomitant variations is to study relations maximizing the variability.

Usually at least 100 units (ie subject/records/forms) are required. But, in many clinical studies only one subject is available. When this is the case, measurements can be repeated in different moments, trying to maximize the variability. For example, if we want to study what is concomitant to our headaches, we keep track at regular intervals of all what we think might be related to this situation. For example, each evening we fill a form in which we provide a subjective measurement of the headache, plus what we ate, what we watched on TV, our feelings, etc. When a sufficient number of forms (possibly more than 100) is filled we can process them.

Data can be collected in various ways: nominal, ordinal, interval and ratio.

1. *Nominal* or categorical data, are made of mutually exclusive modalities. For example: marital status, nationality.
2. *Ordinal* data, are variables where the order matters but not the difference between values. For example, if we ask patients to express the amount of pain they are feeling on a scale of 0 to 10. A score of 7 means more pain than a score of 5, and 5 is more than a score of 3. But the difference between 7 and 5 may not be the same as that between 5 and 3. The values simply express an order, a progression.
3. *Interval* data, are variables where the difference between two values is meaningful. For example the difference between 1 meter and 2 meters is the same difference as between 3 and 4 meters. That is, numbers are spaced always by the same measuring unit.
4. *Ratio* data have all the properties of interval variables, but have also a clear definition of the zero value. Variables like height, weight, enzyme activity are ratio variables. Temperature, expressed in Fahrenheit or Celsius, is not a ratio variable. A temperature of zero degrees on either of those scales does not mean no temperature. Kelvin degrees correspond instead to a ratio variable since zero degrees Kelvin really correspond to no temperature. When working with ratio variables, but not interval variables, it is possible to use divisions. A weight of 4 grams is twice a weight of 2 grams, because weight is a ratio variable. A temperature of 100 degrees Celsius is not twice as hot as 50 degrees Celsius, because

temperatures in Celsius are not a ratio variable. The Celsius scale is an interval variable, whereas the Kelvin scale starts from absolute zero and allows for ratios.

The mathematical operations which can be performed are:

1. in the case of nominal/categorical variables the value is a modality of a list, for example Italy France, Germany. With these variables it is possible only to count the occurrences of the modalities.
2. In ordinal variables the value is a sequence: First, Second, Third; Elementary education, High School, University. It is possible to divide the sequence into high and low, for example high education, low education, or treat each value as a modality (nominal variable). For example, it is possible to count how many people have reached secondary or higher education. It is possible to find which is the level of education attained at least, for example, by 50% of the population. There is an order, a progression, which can be used to create new categories (e.g. low education and high education) or to order the population. Ordinal variables allow for counting and sorting.
3. Interval variables allow to calculate average values and variabilities since they permit the use of additions and subtractions.
4. Ratio variables use the absolute zero value and allow to use divisions and multiplications.

Data can be transformed in one or more dichotomous variables.

1. In the case of nominal variables, the single modality (e.g. single province, nationality, color) can be translated into a dichotomous variable. For example, Italy becomes the Italy dichotomous variable for which the answers can only be: yes or no.
2. Ordinal variables follow a progression. These variables can be treated in the same way as the nominal variables by translating each modality in a dichotomous variable, but it is also possible to translate the information in the form high/low. It is important to note that there is no objective criterion for defining when modalities are considered high or low. For example, in a study concerning university professors the lowest degree of education might correspond to the highest degree in another study which considers the poor population of developing countries. The division of an ordinal variable into a dichotomous variable, must always take into account the context and purpose of the study. In the event that no criterion suggests how to divide between high and low the cut-off point is chosen by balancing the two groups. This is done using the median value.
3. When dealing with interval or ratio variables cut-off values, that mark the transition from low to high values, are generally used. The aim of the researcher and the purpose of data analysis is usually to identify these cut-

off values. It happens frequently that the same variable can be translated into multiple dichotomous variables in order to test which cut-off value best allows to identify a critical value, i.e. a value that indicates the transition from one state to another.

Data is the row material, but not all data is suitable for concomitant variations analyses; only data which can be transformed in the dichotomous form and is gathered in a systematic way can be used. Information which cannot be coded or transformed in the dichotomous form is of little use.

In the late 19th century, Charles Sanders Peirce in *"How to Make Our Ideas Clear"*[30] placed induction and deduction in a complementary rather than competitive context. Secondly, and of more direct importance to scientific method, Peirce put forth the basic schema for hypothesis-testing that continues to prevail today. Peirce examined and articulated the fundamental modes of reasoning that play a role in scientific inquiry, the processes that are currently known as abductive, deductive, and inductive inference:

1. During the *inductive* phase we consciously review the know-how and unsolved problems.
2. During the *abductive* phase unconscious processes take place and lead to intuition which highlights new

[30] Peirce C.S. (1878), How to Make Our Ideas Clear, www.amazon.it/dp/B004S7A74K

hypotheses and solutions.

3. During the *deduction* phase hypotheses are translated into items.

4. During the *validation* phase data is gathered and hypotheses and solutions are tested.

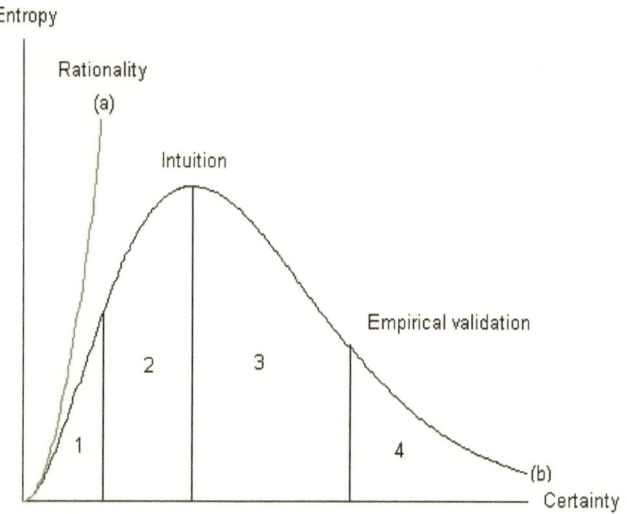

Phases of the process of discovery

One of the most delicate phases is when we translate hypotheses into items (phase 3).

Hypotheses always state a concomitance between two or more variables. In order to test these concomitances it is required to gather data separately. For example if the hypothesis is that loneliness causes anxiety it is wrong to ask: *Loneliness causes anxiety?* because the concomitance between loneliness and anxiety is already given in the item and data analysis will not be able to tell if this concomitance exists.

In order to study the concomitance between loneliness

and anxiety it is necessary to formulate two different items: *Do you feel lonely? Do you experience anxiety?*

Data analysis will tell if these two items (loneliness and anxiety) vary in a concomitant way and are related. It is also important to ask information in a clear and direct way, avoiding negative forms. Each item should contain only one information.

For example the following item is incorrect since it combines State Aid (Yes/No) with Family type (one parent family, two parents family):

Did the family receive State Aid?
- Yes, No,
- It is a one parent family,
- It is a two parents family

The correct formulation is:

Did the family receive State Aid? Yes, No

Family type: One parent, Two parents

Each item (i.e. each variable) must be relative only to one type of information. During data analysis information will be combined and concomitances will be studied.

Items can be divided into key items, explicative and structure items:

1. *key items* are all those variables which describe the topic

under investigation, for example if the study is relative to cancer, key variables will be relative to cancer;

2. *explicative items* are all those variables which might be correlated (linked) to the key variables, for example in the case of cancer it could be the environment, stress, food, and so on;

3. *structure items* are variables such as age, sex, education, profession; variables which are usually used to describe the sample of the study and the context.

In order to choose relevant explicative variables, it can be useful to ask the help of experts who have a good knowledge of the subject. It is also useful to compare different hypotheses. Scientific research is a process of continuous evolution of knowledge which requires the disposition to revisit, change and eventually abandon our beliefs.

Designing a form can be divided in the following steps:

1. declare which is the aim of the study (*key variables*).

2. list all those variables (*explicative variables*) which might be correlated (concomitant) to the key variables. It is very important to keep track of the hypotheses, in this way the interpretation of the results will be straightforward, otherwise it is easy to fall in the trap of paying too much attention to secondary information and produce interpretations which are totally irrelevant and of little scientific value. It is always a good habit to use more items for the same information (redundancy).

3. prepare the form (questionnaire, observation grid, …) and test it in order to assess if it works well or if it can be improved and optimized. It is necessary to continue testing the form until it reaches a standard which we consider acceptable.

Parametric statistical tests are based on the assumption that the variables data in the population are distributed according to the normal (Gaussian) distribution, which in probability theory is a continuous distribution, a function, which allows to calculate the probability that any real observation will fall between any two limits.

On the contrary, nonparametric methods make no assumptions about the distribution of data. Their applicability is much wider than the corresponding parametric methods and, due to the reliance on fewer assumptions, are more robust and simple. Even when the use of parametric methods is justified, nonparametric methods are easier to use and more reliable. Because of their simplicity, results leave less room for improper use and misunderstanding.

In the 1960s Simon Shnoll and co-workers were probably the first scientists to show that the assumption of the normal distribution is only mathematical, and that in life sciences and also in physics it is false.

In a review of studies performed over more than forty

years, Shnoll[31] shows the non-randomness of the fine structure of the distributions of measurements, starting from biological objects and moving into the purely physical domain. The implication is huge: tests based on the assumption of normal random distributions, such as those in the field of parametric statistics, are fundamentally biased and produce results which are often unstable and difficult to reproduce.

The methodology of concomitant variations uses nonparametric statistics, among which the Chi Square (χ^2) is today one of the most widely used statistical indexes. χ^2 calculates the differences between observed frequencies and expected frequencies. In the absence of concomitances χ^2 is equal to 0, whereas in the case of maximum concomitance it is equal to the size of the sample.

The comparison with the χ^2 probability distributions allows to know the statistical significance of the concomitance. Statistical significance indicates the risk which is accepted when we state the existence of the relation. Conventionally concomitances are taken in consideration when the risk is below 1%.

With dichotomous variables concomitances can be accepted with a risk lower than 1%, with χ^2 values greater or equal to 6.635.

When using the methodology of concomitant variations

[31] Shnoll SE, Kolombet VA, Pozharskii EV, Zenchenko TA, Zvereva IM and AA Konradov, Realization of discrete states during fluctuations in macroscopic processes, Physics – Uspekhi 162(10), 1998, pp.1129–1140.
http://ufn.ioc.ac.ru/abstracts/abst98/abst9810.html#d

all variables are translated into the dichotomous form. Crossing two dichotomous variables produces a 2x2 table. If we take, for example, the following variables **A** and **B**:

B	A Yes	No	Total
Yes	18,340	3,241	21,581
No	5,118	29,336	34,454
Total:	23,458	32,577	56,035

the χ^2 value is obtained by comparing the observed frequencies and the expected frequencies.

Expected frequencies are calculated by dividing the product of the total values of row and column by the general total. For the expected frequency of the first cell (Yes / Yes) is:

$$21,581 \text{ x } 23,458/56,035 = 9,034$$

Following this procedure for all the cells of the table we have the following expected frequencies table:

B	A Yes	No	Total
Yes	9,034	12,547	21,581
No	14,424	20,030	34,454
Total:	23,458	32,577	56,035

The Chi Square formula is the following:

$$Chi\ Square = \sum \frac{(f_o - f_e)^2}{f_e}$$

where f_o indicates observed frequencies and f_e expected frequencies

For each cell we calculate the square of the difference between observed frequencies and expected frequencies divided by expected frequencies and we sum the results together.

In this example we obtain a Chi Square value of 26,813, well above the value 6.635 from which the statistical significance of 1% starts.

Since the maximum value of χ^2 varies depending on the number of cases, it is useful to standardize it between 0 and 1. This transformation is known as the *rPhi* and is obtained as the square root of the value of χ^2 divided by the sample size and behaves similarly to Pearson's correlation index.

Correlations/concomitances can be of two types: direct or inverse. If the correlation is directed the two dichotomous variables are concomitantly true or false, whereas if the correlation is inverse one variable is true when the other is false.

Inverse correlations have negative sign (-), whereas direct correlations are shown without sign.

The Sintropia-DS software was developed in order to make the methodology of concomitant variations available. A complete description is available in the help sections of the software, or in the dedicated 2005 issue of the Syntropy Journal.[32]

The first version of Sintropia-DS dates back to 1982, it was distributed with the name DataStat, and extensively used in the Department of Statistics of the University of Rome. Sintropia-DS merges database and statistical analyses (this is the reason of the extension DS: database and statistics).

In order to install Sintropia-DS in your computer: download the zip file from www.sintropia.it/sintropia.ds.zip, copy the folder "Sintropia.DS" from the zip file in the root disk "C:", and find the Sintropia application in the folder Sintropia.DS.

Since this version of the software dates back to 2005 and was developed for Windows-XP, recent version of Windows require that you allow the use of the program.

---

[32] www.sintropia.it/journal

THE COMPASS OF THE HEART

Consciousness, the *"feeling of being alive"* is still a mystery. Neuroscientists assume that consciousness emerges from matter, whereas quantum scientists believe that matter emerges from consciousness.

Luigi Fantappiè and Pierre Teilhard de Chardin described consciousness as a property of the negative time energy. Physical energy can be perceived whereas the non-physical negative time energy can be felt: the head perceives, the heart feels.

We are constantly faced with what the head and the heart say, and we are forced to choose. The heart gives us direction and aim, whereas the head provides tools and experience. Both are needed.

Starting from the dual energy solution the mathematician Chris King[33] speculates that free will arises from the fact that we are faced with bifurcations between information arriving from the past (*entropy*) and feelings arriving from the future (*syntropy*).

These bifurcations entail choices and choosing puts us in a condition of free will.

---

[33] King C.C. (1989) Dual-Time Supercausality, Physics Essays, Vol. 2(2): 128-151;

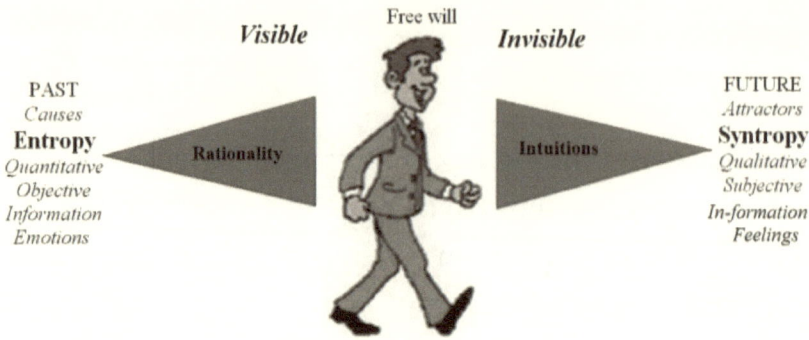

Supercausal model of free will

Since the forward and the backward in time energies are perfectly balanced, similar amounts of information and feelings are received.

This might explain the perfect division of the brain into two hemispheres.

We can replace the previous illustration with that of the two hemispheres of the brain, where the left hemisphere is the seat of the "forward in time" logical reasoning and the right hemisphere is the seat of the "backward in time" intuitive reasoning.

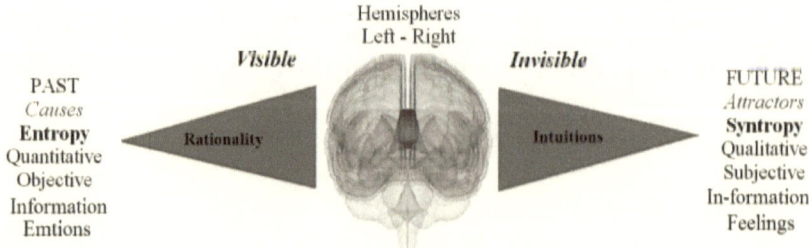

Where the rational-logical thinking is objective and quantitative ant the intuitive thinking is subjective and qualitative.

Syntropy adds to this picture the autonomic nervous systems which allows us to feel the future and describes the mind as organized on three levels:

1. the *conscious mind* which is associated to the head and free will;
2. the *unconscious mind* which is associated to the autonomic nervous system and highly automated processes;
3. the *super-conscious mind* which is linked to the source of syntropy, the attractor, is future oriented and provides direction, purpose and meaning to life.

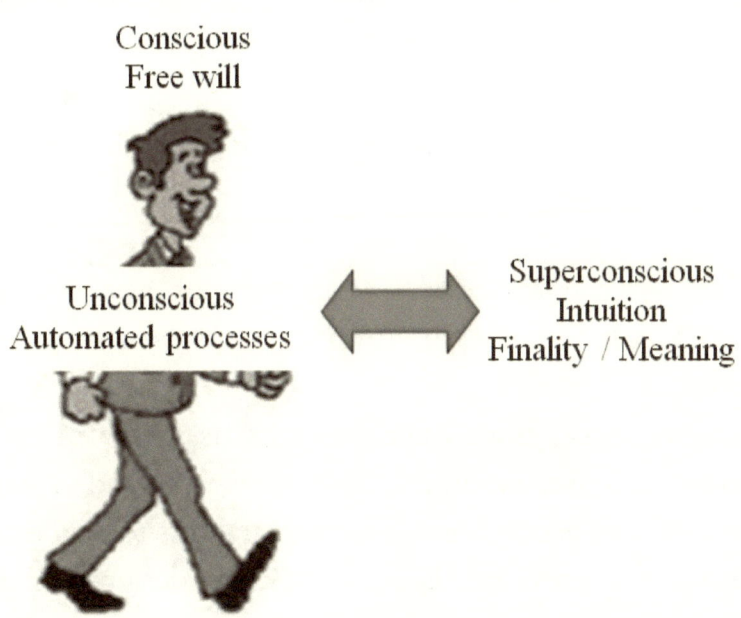

Conscious
Free will

Unconscious
Automated processes

Superconscious
Intuition
Finality / Meaning

The *conscious mind* on which we are tuned during the time we are awake, connects us to the physical reality. The conscious mind chooses between feelings that come from the autonomic nervous system, i.e. the unconscious mind, and information that comes from the physical plane of reality. This continuous state of choice is at the basis of free will.

The *unconscious mind* governs the vital functions of the body, therefore called involuntary, such as heartbeat, digestion, regenerative functions, growth and reproduction.

In addition, it implements highly automated programs, which allow us to perform many complex tasks, without having to think continuously about them, such as walking, riding a bicycle, driving, etc.

The autonomic nervous system supplies the body with syntropy and it is therefore the seat of feelings that inform us about the connection with the attractor. The unconscious mind can be accessed during dreams, or using techniques of relaxation and altered states of consciousness such as hypnotic trance.

The *superconscious mind* is our attractor, the source of syntropy, which guides us towards the most advantageous options.

The superconscious mind provides us with a mission, a purpose, and uses intuitions, insights, dreams and visions. It provides intelligence, knowledge and answers to problems. It leads towards more intelligent and perfect designs which are the outcome of the contribution of all the individuals who share the same attractor.

The autonomic nervous system automatically and unconsciously regulates the vital functions of the body, without the need for any voluntary control.

Almost all the visceral functions are under the control of the autonomic nervous system which is divided into the sympathetic and parasympathetic systems. The nerve fibers of these systems do not directly reach the organs, but stop first and form synapses with other neurons in structures called ganglia, from which other nerve fibers form systems, called plexuses, which reach the organs. The sympathetic part of the system is close to the spinal ganglia and forms synapses together with longitudinal fibers, in a tree called the paravertebral chain. The parasympathetic system forms synapses away from the spine and closer to the organs it controls. The ganglia of the sympathetic system are distributed as follows: 3 pairs of intracranial ganglia, located along the trigeminal, 3 pairs of cervical ganglia connected to the heart; 12 pairs of dorsal ganglia connected to the lungs and the solar plexus, 4 pairs of lumbar ganglia that are connected through the solar plexus to the stomach, small intestine, liver, pancreas and kidneys, 4 pairs of ganglia in connection with the rectum, bladder and genital organs.

For a long time it was believed that there was no relationship between the brain and the sympathetic system, but today we know that this relationship exists, is strong and that the brain can act directly on the organs through the mediation of the solar plexus. There is therefore a link between mental states and physical states. For example, sadness acts on the solar plexus through the sympathetic system, generating a vasoconstriction due to the contraction of the arterial system. This contraction caused by sadness hinders blood circulation, thus also affecting digestion and respiration.

People commonly refer to the heart and not to the solar plexus. However, from a physiological point of view, the organ that allows us to perceive our inner feelings is the solar plexus.

Syntropy nourishes the vital functions and is a converging energy that propagates from the future, consequently when the inflow of syntropy is good we feel warmth (ie energy concentration) and well-being in the thoracic area of the autonomic nervous system.

On the contrary, when the inflow is insufficient we feel emptiness, pain and anxiety.

These sensations work like the needle of a compass which points towards the source of syntropy (ie life energy).

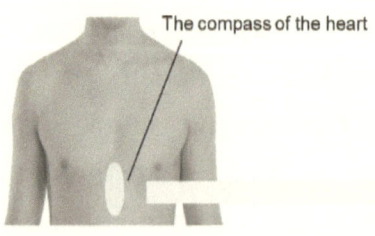

The compass of the heart

The *Attractor*

Unfortunately most people are unaware of how the compass of the heart works and their main concern is to avoid suffering and the unbearable feeling of anxiety. This explains, for example, the mechanism of drug addiction. Substances that act on the autonomic nervous system, such as alcohol and heroin, causing feelings of warmth and wellbeing similar to those that we experience when there is a good inflow of syntropy, can soon become vital.

The compass of the heart points to the source of syntropy, but drugs, alcohol and whatever we use to sedate our suffering reduces our possibility to use the compass of the heart and chose what is beneficial for life.

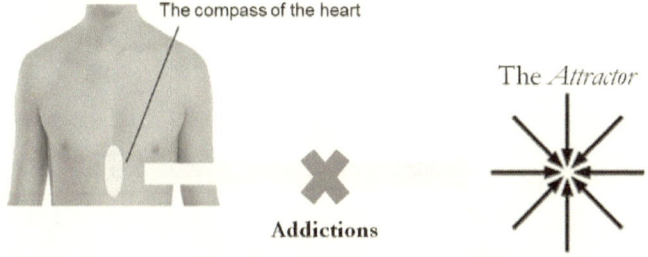

The compass of the heart

The *Attractor*

Addictions

In order to improve the flow of syntropy and promote wellbeing it is therefore essential to abandon any kind of addiction.

While the brain is made of gray matter outside and white matter inside, exactly the opposite is observed in the solar plexus. The gray matter is made up of nerve cells that allow us to think, the white matter is made of nerve fibers, cell extensions, which allow us to feel.

The solar plexus and the brain are the opposite of each other and represent two polarities: the emitter pole and the absorber pole. The same duality that is found between entropy and syntropy.

The solar plexus and the brain are closely connected and from a phylogenetic perspective the brain has developed from the solar plexus. Between the brain and the solar plexus there is a specialization of functions that are completely different and that can only occur when these two polarities are integrated and work in harmony, producing results that are quite extraordinary.

Experiments show that syntropy acts mainly on the solar plexus and is perceived as warmth and well-being. On the contrary, the lack of syntropy is perceived as emptiness and suffering.

Since syntropy propagates backwards in time, feelings of warmth and emptiness help us feel the future and orient our choices towards advantageous goals. The following examples provide some insights into the implications of this backward in time flow:

1. The article *"In Battle, Hunches Prove to be Valuable"*, published on the front page of the New York Times on July 28, 2009, describes how experiences associated with intuitions and premonitions helped soldiers save themselves: *"My body suddenly became cold; you know, that feeling of danger, and I started screaming no-no!"* According to syntropy, the attack happens, the soldier experiences fear and death and these feelings of distress propagate backward in time. The soldier in the past feels these as

premonitions and is driven to take a different decision, thus avoiding the attack and death. According to the New York Times article, these premonitions have saved more lives than the billions of dollars spent on intelligence.

2. William Cox, conducted studies on the number of tickets sold in the United States for commuter trains between 1950 and 1955 and found that in the 28 cases where commuter trains had accidents, fewer tickets were sold[34]. Data analysis was repeated verifying all possible intervening variables, such as bad weather conditions, departure times, day of the week, etc. But no intervening variable was able to explain the correlation between reduced ticket sales and accidents. The reduction of passengers on trains that have accidents is strong, not only from a statistical point of view, but also from a quantitative point of view. According to syntropy, Cox's discoveries can be explained in this way: when people are involved in accidents, the feelings of pain and fear propagate backward in time and can be felt in the past in the form of presentiments and premonitions, which can lead to the decision not to travel. This propagation of feelings can therefore change the past. In other words, a negative event occurs in the future and informs us in the past, through our inner feelings. Listening to these feelings can help us decide differently and avoid pain and suffering in our future. If we listen to the inner voice, the future can change for the better.

---

[34] Cox WE (1956), *Precognition: An analysis*. Journal of the American Society for Psychical Research, 1956(50): 99-109.

3. Among many possible examples: on May 22, 2010 an Air India Express Boeing 737-800 flying between Dubai and Mangalore crashed during landing, killing 158 passengers, only eight survived the accident. Nine passengers, after check-in, felt sick and could not get on board.

In this regard, the neurologist Antonio Damasio, discovered that people with decision making deficit show knowledge but not feelings. Their cognitive functions are intact, but not the emotional ones. They have normal intellect, but are unable to make appropriate decisions. The alteration of feelings causes a myopia towards the future.

Feelings of warmth point to the path that leads to well-being and to what is beneficial to life. It is therefore good to choose according to these inner feelings.

When we converge towards the attractor feelings of warmth inform that we are on the right path, on the contrary when we diverge we feel void and anxiety.

Intuitions arise from the ability to feel the future and are based on inner feelings not contaminated by drugs, alcohol, habits and fears.

Henri Poincaré, one of the most creative mathematicians of the last century, observed that when faced with a new problem whose solutions can be countless, a rational approach is initially used, but being unable to arrive at the result another type of process is activated.

This process selects the correct solution among the endless possibilities, without the help of rationality.

Poincaré called it intuition (combining the Latin words *in*=inside + *tueri*=glance), and was struck by the fact that they are always accompanied by experiences of truth, beauty, warmth and well-being in the thoracic area:[35]

> *"Among the large number of possible combinations,*
> *almost all are without interest or utility.*
> *Only those that lead to solving the problem*
> *are illuminated by an interior experience of truth and beauty."*

For Poincaré, intuitions require attention and sensitivity to these inner feelings of truth and beauty, which connect us to the future, to the intelligence of syntropy.

Robert Rosen (1934-1998), theoretical biologist and professor of biophysics at the Dalhousie University, in his book *Anticipatory Systems*[36] wrote:

> *"I was amazed by the number of anticipatory behaviors observed at all levels of the organization of living systems (...) that behave like real anticipatory systems, systems in which the present state changes according to future states, violating the law of causality according to which changes depend exclusively on past or present causes. We try to explain these behaviors with theories and models that exclude any possibility of anticipation. Without exception, all biological theories and models are classic in the sense that they seek only causes in the past or present."*

---

[35] Henri Poincaré, *Mathematical Creation*, from Science et méthode, 1908.
[36] Rosen R (1985) *Anticipatory Systems*, Pergamon Press, USA 1985.

To make anticipatory behaviors consistent with the idea that causes must always precede effects, predictive models and learning processes are taken into account. But anticipatory behaviors are found also in the simpler forms of life, such as cells, without neural systems, and in these cases it is difficult to sustain the hypothesis of predictive models or learning processes. Furthermore, they are also observed in macromolecules and this excludes any possible explanation based on innate processes due to natural selection. Rosen concludes that a new law of causality is needed to explain the anticipatory behaviors of living systems.

A very important example was provided by Steve Jobs, the founder of Apple Computer.

Steve Jobs had been abandoned by his natural parents and this was the drama that accompanied him throughout his life. He was tormented and never accepted being abandoned.

He left university during the first year and ventured to India to find his inner self.

He discovered a completely different vision of the world that marked his change:

"in the Indian countryside people do not let themselves be guided by rationality, as we do, but by intuitions."

He discovered intuitions, a very powerful faculty, very developed in India, but practically unknown in the West.

He returned to the United States convinced that intuitions were more powerful than intellect. To cultivate intuitions it was necessary to live a minimalist life, reducing entropy as much as possible. He became a vegan, refused alcohol, tobacco and coffee, began to practice Zen meditation and had the courage not to be influenced by the judgment of others.

He always tried to reduce entropy to the point that it took him more than 8 months to choose the washing machine. He absolutely had to find the one with the lowest energy consumption and maximum efficiency. He lived in a thrifty way, a life so essential and austere that led his children to believe he was poor.

The way he lived was the result of his need to focus on the heart, on inner feelings. He avoided wealth because it could distract him from the voice of the heart. He was one of the richest men on the planet, but he lived like a poor man! From a syntropic perspective, his minimalist choices allowed intuitions to emerge, becoming the source of his innovations and wealth.

Jobs opposed marketing studies, as he said that people don't know the future. Only intuitive people can feel the future.

When he returned from India he saw an electronic board at his friend Steve Wozniak's house and he had the intuition of a computer that could be held in one hand. He asked Wozniak to develop a prototype of a personal computer, which he named Apple I. He managed to sell a few hundred and this sudden success gave him the impetus to develop a more advanced model, suitable for ordinary people, which he called Apple II.

Jobs was not an engineer, he had no scientific or technical mind, he was simply an artist! What do computers have to do with his life? Jobs had nothing to do with electronics, but his intuitive abilities showed him a goal, an object of the future. Thirty years earlier, in 1977, he had sensed a pocket computer that combines aesthetics, simplicity, technology and minimalism! He felt the need for a product that, in addition to being technologically perfect, had to be also beautiful and simple!

His obsession with beauty and simplicity led him to devote an enormous amount of time to the details of the Apple II. It had to be beautiful, silent and at the same time essential and simple! It was an unprecedented commercial success that made Apple Computer one of the leading global companies.

Jobs noticed that when the heart gave him an intuition, it turned into a command he had to follow, regardless of the opinions of others. The only thing that mattered was finding a way to give shape to the intuition.

For Jobs, the vegan diet, Zen meditation, a life immersed in nature, abstention from alcohol and coffee were necessary to nourish his inner voice, the voice of his heart and strengthen his ability to intuit the future.

At the same time, this caused great difficulties. He was sensitive, intuitive, irrational and nervous. He was aware of the limitations that his irrationality caused him in handling a large company, such as Apple Computer, and chose a rationalist manager to run the company: John Sculley, a famous manager he admired but with whom he entered continually in conflict, to the point that in 1985 the board of directors decided to fire Jobs from Apple, the company he had founded.

Apple Computer continued to make money for a while with the products designed by Jobs, but after a few years the decline began and in the mid-1990s it came to the brink of bankruptcy. On December 21, 1996, the board of directors asked Jobs to return as the president's personal advisor. Jobs accepted. He asked for a salary of one dollar a year in exchange for the guarantee that his insights, even if crazy, were accepted unconditionally. In a few months he revolutionized the products and on September 16, 1997 he became interim CEO.

Apple Computer resurrected in less than a year. How did he do it?

He said we should not let the noise of others' opinions dull our inner voice. And, more importantly, he repeated that we must always have the courage to believe in our heart and in our intuitions, because they already know the future and know where we need to go. For Jobs, everything else was secondary.

Being interim has marked all his new products. Their name had to be preceded by the letter *i*: *i*Pod, *i*Pad, *i*Phone and *i*Mac.

Jobs's children believed he was poor. They often asked him:

"Daddy, why don't you take us to one of your rich friends?"

He talked about important business walking in parks or in nature. To celebrate a success, he invited employees to restaurants for $10 per person. When he made a gift he collected flowers in a field. He wore the same clothes for years. Despite the immense riches he had!

He was convinced that money was not his, but that it was a tool to reach the end.

At the time of Apple I, he repeated that his mission was to develop a computer that could be held in one hand and not to get rich. For him money was exclusively a tool.

The ability to feel the future was the source of Jobs' wealth. It was the ingredient of his creativity, genius and innovation.

Einstein repeated that:

"the intuitive mind is a sacred gift and the rational mind is its faithful servant. But we have created a society that honors the servant and has forgotten the gift."

Zen meditation helped Jobs calm his mind and move the attention to the heart.

In his lectures he used to say that almost everything, expectations, pride and fears of failure, vanish in the face of death. He emphasized the centrality of death and the fact that when we are aware of dying we pay attention only to what is really important. Being constantly aware that we are destined to die is one of the most effective ways to understand what is really important and to avoid the trap of attaching ourselves to materiality and appearance. We are already naked in the face of death. Since we must die, there is no reason not to follow our heart and do what we have to do.

Jobs believed in the invisible and in synchronicities. He built the headquarters of Pixar (one of his companies) around a central space, a large square where everyone had to go through or stop if they wanted to eat something or use the services. In this way the invisible world was favored by chance encounters.

According to Jobs, chance does not exist. Chance encounters allow the invisible, to activate intuitions, creativity and synchronicities and make visible what is not yet visible.

Jobs loved to quote Michelangelo's famous phrase:

"In each block of marble I see a statue as if it were in front of me, shaped and perfect in attitude and action. I just have to remove the rough walls that imprison the beautiful appearance to reveal it to others as my eyes see it."

Jobs believed that we all have a task, a mission to carry out. We just need to discover this mission by removing what is not necessary.

Jobs made visible what he had intuited. He died a few months after the presentation of the iPad, the computer that can be held in one hand, the mission of his life.

The life of Jobs testifies that intelligence and creativity come from the future, from the invisible and that we can access the invisible through intuitions.

Jobs showed that the voice of the heart brings the future into the present.

Rainer Maria Rilke said:

The future enters us,
to become us,
long before it happens.

BOOKS

The ASIN code is shown in brackets. It can be used to search for books if you have difficulties. The books are available in all formats. Kindle, Paper Back, Hard Cover and Audio book.

The Attractor (B0GZNHPQF9)
Introduction to Syntropy (B006QHVZPA)
Entropy and Syntropy: from mechanical to life sciences (B06XGV6XMK)
A Syntropic Model of Consciousness (B06XKKCC6F)
The balancing role of Entropy and Syntropy (B00KL4SP70)
The Unitary Theory (B01NCOVYUK)
Teilhard and Fantappiè: the converging evolution (B0H248DPN1)
Retrocausality: Experiments and Theory (B005JIN51O)
Supercausality (B005N5KLCE)
Origin of life, evolution and consciousness in the light of the law of syntropy (B005HADKWS)
The Vital Needs Theory (B006M0L0R4)
The methodology of concomitant variations (B00MOBIGWC)
World War III or Syntropy? (B0FSFC8FBT)
Apocalypse and Syntropy (B0B5RMPGKC)
Syntropy and Homeopathy (B07K5XRQNF)
Bach's flowers remedies, synchronicities and attractors (B086XBFTC1)
Climate Change (B07SRBCZVF)
Are we entering the next ice age? Will humanity survive? (B071FQLX6Z)
Syntropy the Trilogy (B09SQ5DNN7)
Money (B07S3TTS7J)
Depression (B07XGHWZ9G)
Liquidarism, Syntropy and Vital Needs (B07QDGZWPS)
Syntropy, Precognition and Retrocausality (B074W7ZL3J)
The invisible force of love (B01I4S8KV0)
The Path to Happiness (B071YWSK6K)
Colonization of Mars, Ice Age, Biological Teleportation and the Meaning of Life (B095PX92H7)

NOTES

www.ingramcontent.com/pod-product-compliance
Lightning Source LLC
Chambersburg PA
CBHW020541290526
45786CB00002B/987